God After Christendom?

God After Christendom?

Brian Haymes and
Kyle Gingerich Hiebert

CASCADE *Books* • Eugene, Oregon

GOD AFTER CHRISTENDOM?

Copyright © 2017 Brian Haymes and Kyle Gingerich Hiebert. All rights reserved. Except for brief quotations in critical publications or reviews, no part of this book may be reproduced in any manner without prior written permission from the publisher. Write: Permissions, Wipf and Stock Publishers, 199 W. 8th Ave., Suite 3, Eugene, OR 97401.

First published by Paternoster, an imprint of Authentic Media, 52 Presley Way, Crownhill, Milton Keynes, MK8 0ES, UK, 2015.
First published in the USA by Cascade Books, 2017.

Cascade Books
An Imprint of Wipf and Stock Publishers
199 W. 8th Ave., Suite 3
Eugene, OR 97401

www.wipfandstock.com

PAPERBACK ISBN: 978-1-5326-1663-1
HARDCOVER ISBN: 978-1-4982-4050-5

Cataloguing-in-Publication data:

Names: Haymes, Brian | Gingerich Hiebert, Kyle

Title: God after Christendom? / Brian Haymes and Kyle Gingerich Hiebert.

Description: Eugene, OR: Cascade Books, 2017 | Series: After Christendom | Includes bibliographical references and index.

Identifiers: ISBN 978-1-5326-1663-1 (paperback) | ISBN 978-1-4982-4050-5 (hardcover)

Subjects: LCSH: God (Christianity) | Theology, Doctrinal | God—Bible teaching. | Christianity—21st century.

Classification: BT103 H396 2017 (print) | BT103 (ebook)

Manufactured in the U.S.A.

Contents

Series Preface	ix
Preface	xi
Acknowledgements	xiii
Introduction	1

Part One: God in Scripture   7

1. In the Beginning   9
- Clearing the Ground   9
- Appealing to the Bible   13
- God and Creation   14
- God's Sovereignty   16
- God's Great Adventure   17
- The Crucial Great Escape   19
- Covenant and Commandments   20
- Give Us a King   22
- Powerful Prophetic Words   23
- God's Strange Presence   24

2. God with Us   27
- Jesus in Context   27
- Beginning the Ministry   28
- The Kingdom in Conflict   30
- The Disturbing Figure of Jesus   31
- Removing This Dangerous Man   33
- Incarnation and New Creation   34
- The Ascended Lord   36
- The Fullest Revelation of God   39

3. God the Spirit — 44
The Powerful Metaphor of Spirit — 44
The Spirit and Jesus — 46
The Spirit and Disciples — 46
The Acts of the Spirit — 48
Conflict Again — 48
Marks of the New People — 50
The Spirit of Unity and Peace — 52
Discerning the Work of the Spirit — 54
Divine, Holy Spirit of God — 56

Part Two: God in the Living Tradition — 59

4. The Triune God — 61
Gesticulating with Words? — 61
Doctrine and Development — 63
Before and After Nicaea — 66
Analogies of the Trinity — 70
Practising Trinitarian Theology — 72

5. Speaking of God — 75
Speaking of the Incomprehensible God — 75
Attend to the Written Word — 76
The Fundamental Distinction — 77
A Way Out of Silence — 81
The Lost Art of Being a Creature — 84

6. God, Faith and Knowledge — 89
On Knowing What You're Talking About — 89
Listening to and Interpreting Scripture — 91
New Insights — 93
Trusting the Witnesses — 95
Faith – Reason – Practice — 96
Examples of Faith in Practice — 98
The Beginning and the End is Worship — 101

Part Three: Encountering God — 103

7. Experience of God — 105
What is Experience? — 105
Experiencing God Unawares? — 106
Stories in the Bible — 109
Stories Outside the Bible — 110
Analyzing Expeience of God — 111

8. God and Evil — 118
Facing Evil — 118
From Augustine to Auschwitz — 119
Does God Suffer? — 123
Challenging the Suffering God — 125
Redeeming Sorrows — 129

9. God in History — 131
An Audacious Hope — 131
The Beginnings of Eschatology in Scripture — 132
The Apocalyptic Politics of Jesus — 134
People of Hope — 137
Practices of Hope — 140

Conclusion — 142

Endnotes — 147
Bibliography — 159
Index — 167

Series Preface

Christendom was a historical era, a geographical region, a political arrangement, a sacral culture, and an ideology. For many centuries Europeans have lived in a society that was nominally Christian. Church and state have been the pillars of a remarkable civilisation that can be traced back to the decision of the emperor Constantine I early in the fourth century to replace paganism with Christianity as the imperial religion.

Christendom, a brilliant but brutal culture, flourished in the Middle Ages, fragmented in the Reformation of the sixteenth century, but persisted despite the onslaught of modernity. While exporting its values and practices to other parts of the world, however, it has been slowly declining during the past three centuries. In the twenty-first century Christendom is unravelling.

What will emerge from the demise of Christendom is not yet clear, but we can now describe much of Western culture as "post-Christendom."

> Post-Christendom is the culture that emerges as the Christian faith loses coherence within a society that has been definitively shaped by the Christian story and as the institutions that have been developed to express Christian convictions decline in influence.

This definition, proposed and unpacked in *Post-Christendom*, the first book in the After Christendom series, has gained widespread acceptance. *Post-Christendom* investigated the Christendom legacy and raised numerous issues that are explored in the rest of the series. The authors of this series, who write from within the Anabaptist tradition, see the current challenges facing the church not as the loss of a golden age but as opportunities to recover a more biblical and more Christian way of being God's people in God's world.

Series Preface

The series addresses a wide range of issues, including theology, social and political engagement, how we read Scripture, youth work, mission, worship, relationships, and the shape and ethos of the church after Christendom.

Eleven books were published by Paternoster between 2004 and 2016:

- Stuart Murray: *Post-Christendom*
- Stuart Murray: *Church after Christendom*
- Jonathan Bartley: *Faith and Politics after Christendom*
- Jo and Nigel Pimlott: *Youth Work after Christendom*
- Alan and Eleanor Kreider: *Worship and Mission after Christendom*
- Lloyd Pietersen: *Reading the Bible after Christendom*
- Andrew Francis: *Hospitality and Community after Christendom*
- Fran Porter: *Women and Men after Christendom*
- Simon Perry: *Atheism after Christendom*
- Brian Haymes and Kyle Gingerich Hiebert: *God after Christendom?*
- Jeremy Thomson: *Relationships and Emotions after Christendom*

Two of these (*Worship and Mission after Christendom* and *Reading the Bible after Christendom*) were also published by Herald Press.

The series is now in the hands of Cascade Books, who are republishing some of the existing titles and commissioning further titles.

These books are not intended to be the last word on the subjects they address, but an invitation to discussion and further exploration. Additional material, including extracts from published books and information about future volumes, can be found at www.anabaptistnetwork.com/AfterChristendom.

Stuart Murray

Preface

For those trying to make some sense of the quite unlikely majestic ascendency of Christianity to its now ever more visible institutional collapse—in short, the story of Christendom—a belief in the providential nature of God is indispensible. For one thing, it enables a less anxious and more sanguine vision of the meaning and direction of history, particularly in the face of the many different kinds of social, political, economic, and environmental crises with which we are faced today. If it is true, for example, that God became incarnate in history and is at work even now reconciling the world then we are freed from the need to pronounce an absolute verdict on the history of Christianity and from pretending to fully understand how and in what ways the Holy Spirit might reweave the tangled threads of creaturely existence into the tapestry of God's infinite peace. Of course, this emphatically does not free us from the difficult work of discipleship, that is, from feeding the hungry, welcoming the stranger, clothing the naked, sheltering the destitute, comforting those who mourn, binding up that which is wounded, doing good even to our perceived enemies. In the words of the author of the letter to the Hebrews, "as it is we do not yet see everything in subjection . . . but we do see Jesus" (Heb 2:7–8).

Whether we are reflecting on the heights of Christendom or its more recent contemporary downfall, the influence of the distinctly Christian understanding of what it is to be human continues to have a profoundly formative effect on the shape of our imaginations and desires, whether we realize it or not. There will always be a struggle between all our attempts to embody the subversive nature of the gospel and our concrete creaturely lives and institutions that are inextricably bound up with failure. In short, while all of creation has been made new in Christ it is nevertheless still groaning in anticipation of its full glory (see 2 Cor 5:17 and Rom 8:22). This observation is just as true of the time of Constantine as it is today and, likewise, is just as true in the United Kingdom, where this book was originally conceived and written, as it is elsewhere.

We make this observation here for two reasons. First, this book was borne out of a deepening belief that the problems currently facing the church are less about the decline of Christendom and more to do with the triumph of Enlightenment rationality and individualism. Admittedly, this is somewhat of a departure from the view of the majority of authors of the engaging books in the *After Christendom* series. However, it is nevertheless a mark of the influence of such a conception of Enlightenment individualism that the first seven books in the series paid only scant attention to the nature and purposes of God. This book was written to address this widespread forgetfulness, which is by no means confined to a book series, with the conviction that a failure to understand the Christian tradition of speech about God means that we will be seriously impaired to faithfully improvise new expressions of the truth, goodness, and beauty of the gospel. Second, we have elected to republish this book in its original form rather than tweaking this or that example in an effort to update the book for a more North American audience. Though some of the references to current events are, quite naturally, drawn from the social and political landscape of the UK, we are nevertheless convinced that thoughtful and reflective readers on the other side of the Atlantic—and, indeed, elsewhere—will quite readily be able to make connections to their own local contexts. Indeed, a large part of what we are suggesting in the pages that follow is that if we return to the sources of Christian thinking about God—in Scripture and in the living tradition of the church—we become better able to read the signs of our own times, whether we live in Manchester or Minneapolis, in Winchester or Winnipeg. The chapters that follow, then, are less an attempt to diagnose particular problems and much more an attempt to rediscover Christian speech about God and the forms of life that arise as a result of such speech as an immense resource that has the power to orient our lives in an increasingly disorienting world and to enliven our own practices of discipleship.

We are grateful to Cascade Books for thinking that the pages that follow are worth reprinting and to Robin Parry in particular for stewarding our work through the publication process.

Kyle Gingerich Hiebert
Brian Haymes
The Feast of St. Thomas Aquinas, 2017

Acknowledgements

As with all of our labours, our debts are many and we are grateful to a number of friends for helping us with this book. We thank Mike Parsons, Commissioning Editor for Paternoster, for urging us to make sure the book was about God, not God and something else. For us to follow his advice meant a strong focus and we have tried to concentrate on this despite the often enticing temptation to do otherwise. Alan Kreider and Ruth Gouldbourne have read parts of the text and have been both probing in their questions and generous in their encouragement. Their helpful words of advice have meant much to us, not least because we are aware that our approach challenges some of the assumptions of the series. In this respect, we also offer our thanks to Stuart Murray, the General Editor of the 'After Christendom' series, for welcoming our contribution to the series. We are particlarly grateful to Trisha Dale for her helpful and clarifying editorial work on the manuscript. We are also indebted to the members of the South Manchester Anabaptist Study Group. This very diverse gathering of teachers, nurses, retailers, pastors and administrators, from several different churches and traditions, have been willing to read chapters with us and offer very helpful comments and criticisms. The eagerness and care with which they engaged our work has been an inspiration to us, and for them to have shared the task of writing with us has been an experience we cherish. However, none of the above are to blame for any mistakes that follow, these are all our own.

Introduction

We're told by Plato, that man, in times of yore,
Wings gorgeous to his glorious body wore,
That all attacks he could unhurt sustain,
By death ne'er conquered, ne'er approached by pain.
Alas, how changed from such a brilliant state!
He crawls 'twixt heaven and earth, then yields to fate.
Look round this sublunary world, you'll find
That nature to destruction is consigned.
– Voltaire (1694–1778)[1]

During the morning of 1 November 1755, a national holiday still celebrated as All Saints' Day, the unthinkable took place. A massive earthquake struck off the coast of the flourishing, opulent and populous city of Lisbon, triggering destruction on a scale hitherto unknown. The pink marble palaces and multistorey stone houses that sprawled across seven hills at the mouth of the River Tagus were swallowed up, their dust rising to blot out the daylight, while the narrow medieval streets were briefly transformed into living arteries strewn with wreckage and corpses from the ensuing tsunami. The Reverend Charles Davy, who survived the quake and tsunami, vividly describes the aftermath this way:

> The whole city appeared in a blaze, which was so bright I could easily see to read by it. It may be said without exaggeration, it was on fire at least in a hundred different places at once, and thus continued burning for six days together, without intermission, or the least attempt being made to stop its progress. It went on consuming everything the earthquake had spared, and the people were so dejected and terrified that

few or none had courage enough to venture down to save any part of their substance; every one had his eyes turned towards the flames, and stood looking on with silent grief, which was only interrupted by the cries and shrieks of women and children calling on the saints and angels for succor.[2]

While Lisbon burned, the rest of Europe, North Africa and even places as far flung as the Caribbean felt the effects of the elemental violence unleashed beneath the ocean floor.

While Voltaire was certainly no friend of Christianity, understanding himself rather as a classical deist, that is, possessing a rational belief in a god who has established the universe and its processes but also as one that has no active relationship with creation, the questions he asks and the god he derides raise the kinds of questions about God with which we continue to be confronted. Indeed, other major earthquakes, in Indonesia (2004), Haiti (2010) and Japan (2011), have captured our collective attention and drawn us again, and again, and again to the question of God. Not that Voltaire's questions will be our questions, which could hardly be the case if what follows purports to be about a god who is anything more than a grand cosmic voyeur. Although Voltaire's questions are not germane to the Christian theological tradition of thinking about God, that his questions continue to captivate us is not wholly problematic. For one thing, they are buoyed by the same rage for justice that is at the heart of the Christian gospel. And for another thing, they embody in some fashion ways of speaking that are familiar to us. At least part of what we shall be suggesting in what follows, however, is that the task of Christian discipleship today is about the business of unlearning some of these familiar ways of speaking about God.

So what are our questions if Voltaire's will not do? And why have we insisted on a question mark in our title? A word about how this book sits within the 'After Christendom' series is in order here. To put it simply, we have questions about the usefulness of the idea of Christendom and how it is sometimes employed. Blunt instruments may not always do their job as carefully as is required and, in consequence, good material may be damaged beyond recognition. If we go back to the fourth century and the consequences of the Emperor Constantine's affirmation

Introduction

of the Christian Faith as the 'official' faith of the Roman Empire we have a prime illustration of what has commonly come to be known as Christendom, sometimes also referred to as Constantinianism. As one of the most articulate critics of the consequences of Constantinianism, John Howard Yoder has offered this definition:

> The identification of church and world in the mutual approval and support exchanged by Constantine and the bishops. The church is no longer the obedient suffering line of the true prophets; she has a vested interested in the present order of things and uses the cultic means at her disposal to legitimate that order. She does not preach ethics, judgment, repentance, separation from the world; she dispenses sacraments and holds society together. Christian ethics no longer means the study of what God wants of man [sic]; since all of society is Christian (by definition, i.e. by baptism), Christian ethics must be workable for all of society. Instead of seeking sanctification, ethics becomes concerned with the persistent power of sin and the celebration of the lesser evil; at the best it produces Puritanism, and the worst simple opportunism.[3]

So it is commonly argued that, in 'Christendom', people are Christians by virtue of their citizenship, not by conviction of the Holy Spirit. They are most likely to be Christian only in name, being baptized and made a member of the church without their own initiative. In 'Christendom', so the argument goes, both church and nation have roles to play but they live as one unified social unit, mutually supportive since they are, in fact, coterminous. The nation has a religion. The church is established, protected and supported by law. This is what lies behind the assertion, still sometimes made, that Britain, for example, is a Christian nation. Fundamentally we think 'Christendom', if we must use the term at all, is best employed as a dangerous term, one that expresses the constant temptation of the church to seek secular influence and power, to take control over the shaping of human society. In this sense, Christendom does not refer only to one extended moment in history surrounding the Emperor Constantine but to an attitude within the church which calls into question the sovereignty of God in all human affairs. Christendom in any form and place is a failure to be faithful to the calling of the church to share the mission of the Triune God.

Therefore, while we acknowledge that this narrative has some useful traction in contemporary Christian thinking, we are not as convinced that the 'post-Christendom' narrative continues to be as useful a description of where we are as perhaps it once was. In any event and especially for the purposes of our present enquiry, the question of God remains the crucial one, whether 'Christendom' is dead or not, and the issue is one of discernment. As will become clear throughout the book, our theological reading of 'the signs of the times' leaves us far less certain that 'post-Christendom', however open-ended a notion, is a particularly helpful one at the present moment.

To cite but one example, we are not at all convinced that it can give an adequately thick description of the recent rise of atheist churches in London.[4] While it is certainly the case that the existence of an atheist church would have been an impossibility in medieval Europe, we are not at all clear that the existence of one in Islington, and now in other places in the West, is proof that we are living in 'post-Christendom'. On the contrary, we are convinced that the existence of atheist churches (interestingly not atheist mosques or atheist synagogues), in whatever heterodox or secularized guise, is evidence of the continuing influence of Christianity in and on contemporary arrangements of power. Moreover, the public figures with whom we might associate these atheist movements – in this context we think especially of Alain de Botton who has suggested the construction of secular cathedrals – are in fact nothing new but are part of a long tradition that stretches back through Nietzsche, Voltaire and Machiavelli, among others.[5] That this tradition of 'enlightenment' predates the Reformation should at least give us pause and cause us to wonder to what extent the vestiges of 'Christendom' are still with us in powerful ways we might not immediately recognize.

Indeed, the involvement of Christianity in UK politics is not simply a matter of lip service to a bygone era as if we are still suffering from a medieval hangover. The political language in the UK of 'the Big Society' with its notions of subsidiarity and mutuality suggests clear association with the rich tradition of Catholic social teaching. Further, in both Europe and America there are urgent discussions about overcrowded prisons and the policies of retributive justice they represent. Along with issues of prison reform there are also explorations and experiments in restorative justice, much of which owes a great deal to the tradition of Christian thought on these matters reflected in the present practices of Christian groups and churches.[6]

Having sounded this note of dissent, we would not wish to deny for a moment that a critique of the church's collusion with coercive power is not important or necessary. The Mennonite theologian A. James Reimer sums this up well:

> There is no denying the power of Yoder's critique of Constantinianism and the 'fall of the church.' It is a message that is not original with Yoder, and one that the church caught in civil religion needs to hear over and over again. But there is an injustice to history, including the Constantinian era, that is committed by Yoder and others for whom 'Constantinianism' is a shibboleth for all that is bad. The third and fourth centuries were a time of great upheaval and diversity. There were many serious Christians, including theologians, clerics, and statesmen, who were attempting to address the profound issues raised by their cultures in the light of the gospel. One cannot dismiss the working of the divine in the movements of history, even in its most unlikely places and persons (like Constantine).[7]

We think there is wisdom in this approach. For our purposes, what matters, as Oliver O'Donovan astutely highlights, 'is not to be *for* Christendom or *against* it – what earthly point could there be in either of these postures? – but to have such a sympathetic understanding of it that we profit from its achievements and avoid repeating its mistakes'.[8] As such, the term 'Christendom' itself will appear only infrequently in what follows as our primary concern is with what has happened and is happening to belief in God through all these changes. Whether Christendom ever existed, or continues or is winding up, the crucial questions for the church have to do with God and our calling to be God's people. Our focus is squarely focused on God's action in the world, that is, on God's sovereignty. We are not seeking to write a kind of 'history of God', although we shall draw deeply from the story of the church and especially the biblical narrative. Neither are we trying to write a systematic doctrine of God in abstraction from the realities of human experience but we are trying to be consistent and systematic about God's engagement with the world. We are going to ask again, what is the project of God in Trinity? What other expressions of the relationship between God, the church and the world can we discern and learn from? How can all this help us to be faithful in our Christian calling to be the church in the purposes of the Christlike God for the world? How might faithful disciples of Jesus, believing and trusting in God, relate to the political, social, economic, moral and environmental realities of our day? We shall argue that we are part of one continuous narrative, taking our part in a story that begins with God, is told in Scripture and continues even now. Most generally, this book is divided into three parts. We shall begin in Part One by exploring God in Scripture. Who is God in the Christian story? The first chapter is devoted to exploring God the creator, the second to God as giver and gift, and the third to God the Spirit. Part Two is devoted to an exploration of how the God whose story is told in the Bible remains the focal point for confronting new challenges that arise in the course of faithful living. Chapter 4 attends in particular to the crucial doctrine of God as Trinity, which came to be essential for grasping an understanding of God's work of salvation in and for the world. Chapter 5 focuses on what it means to speak of God today while Chapter 6 addresses thorny questions of faith and knowledge. Part Three is given over to an exploration of what it means to encounter the living God. We shall explore what it is to experience God in these changing days, with a particular emphasis on the awesomeness of God, in Chapter 7. Chapter 8 explores the question of God and evil with particular reference to some more recent challenges to the tradition that pose serious questions for our understanding of God. We conclude in Chapter 9 with reflections on God acting in history and the meaning of hope.

In our discussion of the development of doctrine later in the book we will come to see that there is more than one way to speak truthfully of God because all our speaking is constantly revolving around the same subject and looking at it from different angles. As G.K. Chesterton suggests, therefore, saints as radically different as Francis of Assisi and Thomas Aquinas are doing the same work, albeit in different ways.[9] We want to raise this at the outset because the chapters that follow speak in two voices that, although different, are nevertheless trying to say the same thing. Attentive readers will be able to discern a difference between our voices, inflecting as they do the truth of God in different ways.

Introduction

We are not suggesting that the difference in our voices is anything like as stark as the difference between Francis and Thomas, nor are we suggesting any likeness between the two of us and these two saints. Nevertheless, Chesterton's insight remains helpful because at times we will speak with a profound plainness beneath which lies a wealth of theological complexity and at other times complexities will rise to the surface with the intention of pointing us back to the simplicity of God. We do not consider this difference-in-unity a problem, however, because it exemplifies the process of reconciliation that integrates all of creation into the story of God's peace as a *symphonia*.[10] If our voices can in some imperfect way participate together in that grand symphony of praise to God we will judge this to have been a worthwhile endeavour.

We think we are sharing in an important discussion and we are glad you are willing to share it with us. We shall be as positive as we can but are fully aware that any complete and final answer to the questions posed will be beyond us. Therefore, at times we shall be deliberately tentative. Even our strongest affirmations will have a provisionality about them as we are convinced that the deepest meaning of all our talk about God can be spoken with integrity only in the context of faithful discipleship and the wonder of worship.

PART ONE:

GOD IN SCRIPTURE

1.

In the Beginning

I am the Lord your God, who brought you out of the
land of Egypt, out of the house of slavery;
you shall have no other gods before me.

– Exodus 20:2–3[1]

Clearing the Ground

Our theme is the sovereignty of God but before we begin at the beginning, there are two preliminary points we wish to underline. Both of these figure in contemporary debates about God, expressing challenges to any easy uncritical slogans of faith and common naive belief.

First, as a matter of fact, there is no sustained argument in the Bible for the existence of God. 'God' is simply 'there, in the beginning' and God will be there at the end. There is no attempted argument or demonstration of the existence of God on which the whole foundation of belief might be built up, no proof of God. Of course, the Bible contains references to people's struggles to understand the ways of God, to keep faith in God, to maintain some sense of God in worship and trust in God's justice. It recognizes that there are enough problems for faithful people to count as evidence against God. This honest variety of human experience, good and bad, is recognized in the Psalms, for example, with the many different expressions of human response in life before God, but there is no argument to prove the existence of God that does not presume that existence beforehand. This explains why so much of the Bible comes in narrative form, telling stories of the ways God is present to the world rather than offering syllogisms to be logically dissected, discarded or defended. Certainly, the Bible text provides important material for later philosophical debates about God but it is not itself that kind of writing. It comes from faith and is written for faith. Formal intellectual 'belief' in God is not the central focus of the Bible. Indeed it acknowledges that kind of belief which even the demons share (Jas 2:19) but having faith and trust in God is more than any formal belief that there is a God.

This is deeply frustrating for those of our contemporaries who want all claims to knowledge to be provable, empirically demonstrable.[2] They wonder at the sense and sanity of those who will, as it were, base their whole lives upon what they cannot demonstrate and prove! After all, it is on this basic epistemological foundation that the vast and wonderful growth of science has happened and to which we are all indebted. Does it make any sense to trust, even talk about what we cannot prove and show? Of course, such proof or demonstration would have to be in keeping with the object under scrutiny and it is not impossible that some important features of our living cannot supply such conditions of evidence and proof. For example, by what conditions do we say that this picture is truly beautiful or ugly? Perhaps there are none and such judgements are matters of personal taste. Or what about claims that some action is right or wrong? Can we settle these arguments, even engage in them, without taking the concept of moral obligation as a given in human life? Perhaps talk of God is not the only language we use about our life and that of the world that cannot be proved. Perhaps the very varied and rich way the Bible itself speaks about God, with no attempt to build a single systematic foundation, calls us to think hard about our language and its use, an issue of some significance when it comes to God and Christendom. We shall attend to this theme in a later chapter.

Second, not only is there no independent proof but we also find there is no discussion of 'God' in the Bible in abstraction as it were. 'God' is not spoken of in isolation, 'God' as God's own self. 'God' is always God in relating within the Bible story. Thus God is pictured in the setting of the heavenly court, discussing how his purposes might be worked out (Isa. 6:1–8). God is the One who of love and love alone brings human life to being. There are stories picturing God seeking humankind in conversation and partnership (Gen. 3). The only humanity the Bible seems to know is one fundamentally related to God, the God who seeks a partnership with humankind in the divine project for all creation. The biblical word for this is 'covenant', a key word in both Old and New Testaments. Indeed the rich and thick way the Bible speaks of God gives rise to the later development of the doctrine of God in Trinity where relating in outgoing love is the very heart of the divine life, social not solitary. So the God of the Bible is ever engaged with the history and nature of the world, with creation. It is possible to think of and define the divine as separate from the world of matter and politics as various other faith traditions do. But this is not the tradition of the Christian Scriptures. We shall see how acknowledging this relating and how it happens is a very important matter in all discussion about the form of relating called Christendom.

Appealing to the Bible

Christendom is 'the identification of church and world in . . . mutual approval and support'.[3] In Christendom, church and state are allies and share mutual responsibilities and interests. We shall discover that both advocates and critics of Christendom appeal to the Bible to support their claims. Reading the Bible is not always the simple matter it can be taken to be, for the truth is that all of us come to the book, any book, with our own thoughts, prejudices and ways of looking at the world. Metaphorically, we all read through spectacles and we two white western males will try to be aware of that fact as we go into this study. This does not mean that any sense readers claim to make of the Bible text is automatically valid and allowed, as if the meaning of a biblical passage it what I say it is and that's that! By contrast, it does mean the way of reading most likely to be helpful is marked by a kind of corporate modesty, an openness and readiness to have our assumptions challenged. It implies a reading and thinking together. Indeed, the Bible itself contains the penetrating question to put to all theologies, to all attempts to classify 'God' under a single concept when it asks, 'To whom then will you compare me, or who is my equal? says the Holy One' (Isa. 40:25). This is not to say that the stance the

Bible takes is one of great cautiousness about talk of God to such an extent that we humans can have nothing to say about God and had best keep silent. The Bible makes strong affirmations about who God is and what God is doing in history, such as the fundamental assertion of the apostolic faith that 'it is the God who said, "Let light shine out of darkness", who has shone in our hearts to give the light of the knowledge of the glory of God in the face of Jesus Christ' (2 Cor. 4:6).

We could, at this point, try simply to set out to show how some Christians use the Bible to appeal to their support for the concept of Christendom and, by contrast, how others rejoice in the demise of Christendom by also appealing to the Bible. It is tempting to take this path because then, at least for those who take the biblical text as authoritative, we could make some judgement as to which one or other is true or false. We could claim to have marked out 'the biblical view' and, assuming there was such a view, that would be no insignificant achievement, a useful contribution to current debates. That the Bible has one unified view on such questions is an assumption many Christians have and share. But, suppose the assumption is wrong; suppose the Bible itself shows a diversity in these matters; suppose the Bible contains material for both arguments, that forms of church and nation relations that find expression in Christendom and other arguments against such alliances are to be found within the text? This is at least possible given the wide range of historical contexts out of which the biblical texts come, covering hundreds of years. Might this suggest that God acts and responds in history in particular ways and is not to be thought of as some universal concept? We think this is the case and so it is what we shall explore in the rest of this chapter.

Thus far we have been clearing the ground, as it were. Let us now turn and do what the Bible itself does, and give our attention to some particular events and affirmations, by way of identifying what relationship is being described between God and the world, God's sovereignty, and God and those called to be God's people.

God and Creation

First, God and what we call creation. There are so many issues here that we shall give a whole chapter over to them later in the book but for the moment we affirm God's relationship to all that is and that God's activity is continuing. We are not offered a scientific account of the origin of the universe but what is affirmed is the rule of God over all things. God is the One in whom and through whom all things live and move and have their being. The creation stories vary. On the one hand, God calls life into being *ex nihilo*, out of nothing, for there is and was nothing before God. Creation is not a matter of God coercively imposing form on matter. On the other hand, God's creative work brings order out of chaos. God's creativity cannot be reduced to one single past act as it were but rather describes God's continuing relationship to all that is. God loves matter and is ever creating new worlds. Thus it was the faith of Israel that God was the sovereign Lord of creation, that what God had brought forth was good, that God sustains it all in being and seeks partners to bring it to what God calls it to be. God is related therefore to the world but not to be identified with it. God is not a 'nature deity'. Rather God is Lord of nature as of its history. As the Bible tells the stories of beginnings in Genesis it is clear that issues of authority, sovereignty, dominion, stewardship and power are being addressed. These political terms, ones dear to Christendom, are there 'in the beginning'.

God engages with whatever threatens the divine gift of life. So any chaos is challenged, and decay, disaster and death are taken up into God's creative purposes but not without humankind. The rule of God over creation is not so absolute that everything that happens does so because of God's will. Creation at its best sings God's praise in delight, the heavens tell the glory of God (Ps. 19:1). But when things go wrong, the floods rise, the tectonic plates slip, the volcanos blow, then God does not stop that creative care but seeks in and through it all to bring new beginnings and liberation for nature and humankind. God's authority over creation is marked by love and longing, not power and control. Such it appears is something of the rule of God. The divine control over all things is gentle, persuasive, loving, not that of threat or naked power. God gives, sustains, rescues and nurtures life, and the way of God's actions is not like the brutality we can show nature and one another.

But what of those stories when God sends floods, makes the

tempest blow, and causes the fire to fall (Ps. 18:7–15)? This sounds like real power. Certainly the One whom winds and waves obey is not like us who have real issues about our lack of climate control. Given our understandings of how the world of nature 'works', and the measure of independence God gives to all that is, it is hard to think that God uses nature to punish or enhance human life. Do drought conditions mean that God is displeased, or that those suffering are serious sinners getting what they deserve? That might be the way some people thought but Jesus seems to be more circumspect. He taught that God sends the rain on the just and the unjust – and life's like that (Matt. 5:45). In many biblical stories where God seems to shape nature it is to his purposes of liberation for humankind. It is not helpful to think of God's control over nature in ways we imagine absolute authoritative control should be, with force and power. Would human life be possible if God were like that?

We must leave these issues here for the moment, with the promise that they shall receive more attention in a later chapter. The Bible's picture seems to be that God rules but not in ways that are our ways (Isa. 55:8–9). This warning may prove to be more important than we realize.

God's Sovereignty

Let us now turn to focus on the theme of sovereignty in human affairs. How does the Bible see God the creator again acting in these situations? We shall need to move carefully and slowly because the answer may be more complex than we wish. That God acts in history is a conviction of traditional Christian belief. Let's put aside for the moment the demanding philosophical questions that raise themselves about such language, to which we shall return in a later chapter, and concentrate on the stories the Scriptures tell and the pictures of divine sovereignty they present.

So, back to the beginning. The opening of Genesis, chapters 1 to 11, it may be argued, act as a prologue to the whole canon of Scripture. In the beginning everything was good. Chaos was held back and beauty and order shaped all that God had made and was making. Then, in the narrative, things start to go wrong. Relationships of joy become broken as Adam and Eve fall out with one another and with God. They hide and the ever-loving God must come seeking and calling for them. 'Where are you?' is one of the questions God persists in asking in the divine quest for humankind. One of Adam and Eve's sons becomes the first murderer, seeking to solve his problem as he saw it by violence. And it goes on, one thing after another. Until, to cut the story short, humankind attempts the impossible, to build a tower, an organization that can compete with God. The tower of Babel (Gen. 11:1–9) may be an expression of human pride encountering God's punishment. Or it may be a picture of human desire for uniformity and sovereignty which stands in contrast to God's gift of diversity in human life. In the latter case, the tower represents human desire for control and if the builders pull it off then there is nothing they might not accomplish, totalitarian rule in fact. So, in the story, God comes spreading confusion of languages, scattering people all over the earth. We might ask, is the story of the tower of Babel one of judgement, or salvation? It will not be the last time such a question is posed of Bible stories of the acts of God. How is this world and its life to be organized? What form of sovereignty will be liberating, fulfilling and saving?

Either way, by the time we reach the end of Genesis 11 we are virtually back to chaos again. What God had made delightful and good is now a mess, with broken relationships, struggle and fear everywhere, a world we recognize. Now what is God going to do? How will God's sovereign will for the world show itself? So we come to one of the foundational stories of the Bible.

God's Adventurous Rescue

God's way of restoring and renewing humankind begins in a particular way, the particularity being significant. A couple, Abram and Sarai, are called by God to begin an adventure, to go to a new land, a good land with God. This is not a matter of God abandoning the world and its people. It is a new initiative, a 'new thing' which we shall often find God doing in his desire to save the world. So, this gracious calling of Abram and Sarai is not to separate themselves from the world but to be a new people, a new politics, in the world. The chaos of Babel is not how it shall be among them. They are invited into this creative hopeful gifted relationship. They are not threatened, nor coerced into response. They are called. Perhaps they were not the first to hear this invitation of God. Who knows? Perhaps others had turned God down, seeking such security and life as they could find in the threatening chaos of political disorder. We do not know.

The story has it that Abram and Sarai are the couple who said 'yes' to God's call and so left their past in search with God for a new future. And why them? We don't know. God loved them and chose them and that's just about all that we can say. God makes it clear that he will stand by them, he will be their God and they shall be God's people (Gen. 12). God will bless them but, and this is really important, in order that through them God's blessing may be known by all peoples, for all the nations. Abram and Sarai are agents with God not just as part of some private sectarian deal for their future but for the future of the whole human race. This may sound a very weird plan to us, even unfairly discriminating. There are serious dangers in the plan, for Abram and Sarai may come to think of themselves more highly than they ought to think, taking airs and graces God did not intend. And anyway, they may prove to be unfaithful to God's calling, seeking their own way in days to come, deserting the divine purpose. But this is God's way, the way of gracious election, the way of covenant promise and the call to faithfulness. It sounds like high risk. Can Abram and Sarai and their descendants be trusted? And will they trust God?

God, it seems, is not going to deal with humankind in general, in the mass, but only through the particular, the personal. The particular may be personal but the scope is purposeful, catholic and universal. This involves vocation and response, free response. God does not threaten or cajole, insisting like some leaders on blind obedience. This is a relationship of trust and, it seems, God is open to bearing the rejection of his will and way, bearing with it and still persisting in the calling of people to share with him the great adventure of the world's creative redemption. And from the first the story makes it obvious that God faces opposition, those who have other plans for the people of the world, who do not like God's politics, God's sovereign way. Another foundational event for Abraham and Sarah (as God renamed them) and their descendants came in a kind of 'head to head' contest between God and those who would thwart God's purposes. Having passed through many adventures, the descendants find themselves in a context which is worsening day by day. They are in Egypt, the most powerful nation of the day, ruled by ambitious Pharaohs. The called and chosen people have become Pharaoh's slaves and his ambitions become an impossible burden to bear. The enslaved people call to their covenant God, to keep his promises, to come and deliver them. So, in the book of Exodus, we meet Moses, one of the Hebrew people. He too is called by God and his task will involve confronting Pharaoh and leading the people in the way of God's liberation.

The Crucial Great Escape

Egypt is the first powerfully organized nation capable of imposing its will on others we meet in the Bible story and its image is not good. This is not to say that Egypt is outside the loving purposes of God. Moses taught, 'You shall not abhor any of the Egyptians, because you were an alien residing in their land' (Deut. 23:7). The Hebrews became a slave people, forced to serve the desires of their masters. The liberty God gave has been taken by another power. In the story of the great escape we call the exodus God acts, sometimes through Moses, to set the people free and call them again to the way of trust and the journey to the promised land. The story might be read as a fundamental struggle between Egyptian government through Pharaoh and God's sovereign way. Whatever the power, God's purposes for his people are triumphant. Egypt can wreak havoc on a slave people but the God of Abraham, Isaac and Jacob, the God who calls Moses, keeps faith. The power of Egypt, even the gods of Egypt, cannot stand against him. Nations may build towers, temples, treasure cities, but all these pass. Only the purposes of God remain. Along with the calling of a people through whom God seeks to bless all people, the story of the exodus from Egypt sets, as it were, a trajectory for biblical faith in God. God saves from institutionalized evil and oppression, but not without human partnership, without Moses and Aaron and a trusting obedient people. In narrative form it becomes a confession of faith:

A wandering Aramean was my ancestor; he went down into Egypt and lived there as an alien, few in number, and there he became a great nation, mighty and populous. When the Egyptians treated us harshly and afflicted us, by imposing hard labour on us, we cried to the Lord, the God of our ancestors; the Lord heard our voice and saw our affliction, our toil, and our oppression. The Lord brought us out of Egypt with a mighty hand and an outstretched arm, with a terrifying display of power, and with signs and wonders; and he brought us into this place and gave us this land, a land flowing with milk and honey. (Deut. 26:5–9).

Covenant and Commandments

An important feature of the covenant bond God initiated with Israel is what we have come to call the Ten Commandments (Exod. 20; Deut. 5). Reading what God commands of the people tempts us to draw a very modern distinction but one which is unhelpful. We think of some commands as strictly religious, others as social, yet more might be thought of as only ceremonial. Thus we divide up what Israel received as one law from the hand of God. In these commandments, faith and living are inextricable. Here is God's way for God's people to live. The first commandment sets the fundamental direction, 'I am the Lord your God, who brought you out of the land of Egypt, out of the house of slavery; you shall have no other gods before me' (Exod. 20:2–3). The great work of deliverance is recalled and the exclusive claim of the liberator is announced. It means that, for Israel, for God's covenant people, all other claims to authority and governance are relativized. This does not mean there might not be other monarchs among the nations, even among the people of Israel, but God alone is the Lord, the God who brings liberation to people trapped in the designs of false pretenders. This is a major theme through the Scriptures. It is an essential element in any definition of God. 'I am the Lord, that is my name; my glory I give to no other, nor my praise to idols' (Isa. 42:8). Any group of people called by this God will clearly have difficulties with other powers who claim more than is their due, who threaten God's total and absolute claim.

We also note at this point the inherently political nature of the commandments in their capacity to shape the life of the community. So, for example, among God's people there will be no bearing of false witness, no robbery, no murder. There is a 'shape' to this community that lives in covenant love with God, under the claims of God. This is no arbitrary matter for in the commands of God is the wellbeing and health of the community. God's great 'words' are intended to bless the common life of those whose calling is to be a blessing to others. God is no proud monarch out to impress others with force, buildings or any other pretentious designs.

The sovereignty of God relativizes all other powers, all other claimants to rule over us. As we noted above, Egypt was the first actual government featured in biblical history. It is a depressing but realistic picture. There is a monarch, Pharaoh, almost divine in self-importance, surrounded by a court of religious and political power. They own slaves and use them tyrannically for building even greater cities. Such was the oppressive nature of this rule that it is no wonder that the slaves cried out for liberation.

We should note that it was not always so in the biblical story of Egypt and God's sovereign rule. Before the story of the exodus, we have the narratives of Joseph, son of Jacob, son of Isaac, son of Abraham. Just how Joseph got into Egypt is not the most edifying of family stories but it is told because it contains the hand and purposes of God. What the brothers of Joseph meant for harm God meant to another purpose (Gen. 45:5). Joseph becomes a key person at a time of severe famine He develops a creative economic administration, saving in the good times so that there will be enough when the crops fail and famine threatens. Joseph is used by God for the purposes of good government and a means of blessing the nations. Good government promotes in this way the compassionate justice of God for all. Here God and those faithful to the divine calling are the means of blessing as God's calling is inseparable from economic and political consequences. It only starts to go wrong when Joseph is forgotten and a new Pharaoh comes asserting personal power and effecting tyranny. So we find, inevitably, a contest between God and Pharaoh. The way the story is told – of Pharaoh's unreasonable demands, of God's call for liberation, of God hardening Pharaoh's heart – implies a struggle for the will of God to be done on earth.

We note that significant place Moses and others play in this, the courageous witness they bear. Does this give an important indication as to how it will always be as God seeks partners to share with him the struggle with other powers who deny human liberation and fulfilment? Is God the saviour always about the task of bringing liberation from demonic institutionalized powers? If so then this means something about the political life of those who are glad to affirm no other gods before God.

Give Us a King

The history of the people of Israel is as mixed as any human history would be. It is never simply the story of human deeds, good and evil. It is always the story of God among this people, keeping covenant promises, and this sometimes leaves an ambiguity in the minds of the readers. As we might expect, the people are not always faithful to their calling. For example, the various tribes that made up the people of Israel could not always be relied upon to pull together and come to each other's need when occasion demanded. In their lack of care one for another they were weakened and vulnerable to the desires and brutality of other nations. This seems to have been behind the popular request for God to give them a king. In military and political terms this seems a not unreasonable request. When such things were hinted at in the time of the judges, Gideon spoke a faithful word when the people called him to be their ruler after a victory over the Midianites and he replied, 'I will not rule over you, and my son will not rule over you; the LORD will rule over you' (Judg. 8:23). Since God is faithful to the covenant and always at work in history, why do the people want another king? Their answer is, 'so that [they] may be like other nations' (1 Sam. 8:19–20). They had forgotten that, in the liberating purposes of God, they were not called to be like the other nations, trusting in kings and weaponry and alliances. They were to be a different people, not like the others. They lived not only for their national interest but in the service of God.

But the people persisted in their request and God gave them their desire. Monarchy began in Israel in spite of the prophets' warnings that it would lead to taxes, warfare, theft of land and liberty (1 Sam. 8:11–18). The experiment of monarchy proved to be a mixed blessing. Certainly there were good kings, whose rule was a blessing to Israel and the nations. God, it seems, was able to use and work through those who recognized the divine sovereignty and lived to serve the divine purpose. God remained sovereign. But God did not override, as it were, the free humanity of those appointed to this high office. So the kings, leaders and judges in Israel turned out to be flawed people, just like the rest of us. They had to learn how to face the temptations which go with power and its desires. They were not always successful in resisting temptation and so Israel became like the other nations with taxes imposed by the king, armies were raised, food supplies controlled, foreign alliances entered into with religious consequences, and all this represented a growing trust in politics and power without calling on the liberating God.

We ought to make special mention of David and the covenant God made with his house. David shows all of those human frailties which go with being a man. He also shows political shrewdness in establishing a strong fortified capital at Jerusalem and bringing to it the ark of the covenant. The city becomes the religious and political centre of the nation's life. David is rarely pictured as the ideal king but there did emerge in Israel the hope that there would come one of David's line whose reign would express the fulfilment of all the promises of God. So the theme of kingship was not lost in Israel. However, it is no surprise that after the exile there was no attempt to reinstate a monarchy.

Powerful Prophetic Words

Two stories help us pick up the emphases of the Old Testament perspectives. One comes from 1 Kings 17. Ahab is king in Israel and Jezebel is queen. Elijah is a prophet, one who hears and speaks the word of God. As such, prophets were a 'destabilizing presence'.[4] Elijah delivers the word announcing a famine whatever the king's plans might be. He is also told to go away, to Zarephath, to the margins of the royal territory to meet with a widow there. She feeds him from a jar of meal that never ran out. The picture contrasts the royal rule which fails the people and the divine word which brings nourishment, even away at the edges of royal influence. The man of God is in solidarity with the marginal and vulnerable in the form of the widow woman. There is much more to this story but the destabilizing presence of the one who lives by the word of the Lord is described in a sharp narrative. And the providential care of God goes way beyond the failure of the king to care for his people. Is it significant that all this happens on the margins of the king's rule?

The second incident is found in Amos 7:10–15. Amos is not one of the 'professional' prophets that may be found in and around the royal court. But he was called of God to the task of prophecy. His message was sharp and piercingly critical of some life in Israel where social and economic injustice was growing. So the priest at Bethel warns Jeroboam the king about this lively critic. He tells Amos to go away, to leave the king's sanctuary where the professionals work to bless the royal house. But Amos speaks only the word of the Lord and if the king and his court are affronted then that is something to do with God's message. Don't blame the messenger who speaks truth to power. Thus royalty is subject to the word of God in the Old Testament as is everyone else. God may use the office of kingship but there can be no uncritical relationship between priest, prophet and monarch.

There are two further aspects of the story of God we need to record in this opening chapter. The fundamental sin of 'the nations' is that of idolatry, the creating of gods. It is a sin which can be the subject of heavy mockery (Isa. 44:9–20). Israel was not above slipping into this sin, giving Jerusalem an idolatrous status as the dwelling of God that would never fall. It was part of the work of the prophet Jeremiah to undo this belief and warn of impending disaster if the people did not keep the covenant. The disaster came and so the people were taken into exile in Babylon, a strange land far from home and, so they supposed, far from God. But it was in this difficult context that they discovered things about God, two of which we mention here.

God's Strange Presence

The first was the realization that God was with them in this strange land where they found it so hard to sing the ancient songs. God was not confined in the temple, not even the land of Israel. They discovered that wherever they go they might find God already there, a truth celebrated in Psalm 139. In fact, God was inescapable if not always obvious. God was never geographically restricted, a truth this demoralized community of Israel was glad eventually to affirm. The second insight was that God shared the suffering humiliation among the nations which the people knew and that such a disaster was not apart from the sovereign rule of God. There came from those years of exile the songs of the suffering servant (Isa. 42:1–4; 49:1–6; 50:4–11; 52:13 – 53:12). No one can be completely sure of the identity of 'the servant', maybe individual, maybe corporate, maybe the nation, but obedient suffering even to death is an essential feature of the servant's calling and mission to the world. The servant gives and lives, suffers and dies for the sake of others in the purposes of God. The redemption of the world is not without sacrifice and suffering.

However, the questions of how social life should be shaped and organized remained. It is no incidental matter to note that nowhere in the story did God compel or threaten Israel. For sure, God would rebuke the people called to covenant trust when they disobeyed. But there was no force, as Israel was never called to force others to their ways of life. If the picture is that the other nations will come to Israel to worship it is for the worship of God alone. Israel was called and lived to serve the purposes of God who loved the world and all its people. They were always God's even when they did not known it (Ps. 24:1).

Israel knew that acknowledgement of God's sovereignty was a blessing. Poor leadership, which usually found expression in false worship, was often a disaster. In such circumstances there was usually a leader or party who thought of themselves more highly than they ought to think, putting themselves above the law of God. On such occasions those faithful to the covenant found themselves at odds with the boastful power. But they were never abandoned by God. He gave them to dream dreams of a different way of life on earth to that of the violence and power struggles they encountered and sometimes shared (Mic. 4:1–4). Close examination of the teaching (Torah) they received in the books of Moses gives any lie to facile suggestions that the Old Testament is the story of a brutal selfish god with no longing for the *shalom* of all the children of the world.[5] It is in the sovereign will for all people that peace and justice embrace one another (Ps. 85:10).

We began with God, creator, liberator, sovereign Lord, whose ways and thought are different from ours. We have noted how God calls humans into a partnership in ordering and enabling creation and all people to be all that they are called to be in the creator's purpose. We have seen how those 'called' are not called to be agents of any nation or empire's policies as submissive unquestioning servants, but to be partners with God and all those God choses to use in the divine purpose. Indeed, such is the sovereign way of God that those outside Israel can sometimes be used to further God's purposes for Israel and therefore for all humankind.[6] Things go awry when the called-out people, let alone the monarchy, forget the absolute nature of the divine calling. Then life is no longer shaped to the will of the liberating God but by other claimants with other agendas. The partnership God seeks becomes distorted by injustice, envy, greed, pride. In the Old Testament story of God, that often led to idolatry and the following of a false cult. Something then has gone seriously wrong. It has been forgotten that we all live *sub specie regni Dei*, under the reign and rule of God.

Before we move on, we return for a moment to our beginning affirmation that there is no attempted proof, no argument, for the existence of God in the Bible. God is simply 'there', not part of a class of beings called gods, not even as the head of that class. This is part of the reason why Israel in worship and life would not speak the name of God, the Holy One. When the sacred name appeared in the Scriptures they vocalized another term, a metaphor from a stock available in common descriptions of gods. Herbert McCabe describes this as God verbally dressed in second-hand clothes that don't fit very well.[7] Any complete identification or description of God is beyond us and any attempt to break the barrier ends only in idolatry. So there is a necessary silence before God, a carefulness about language we shall think about later. For all this caution, however, the Bible is not utterly silent because of the conviction that the unspeakable God is known to us in God's effects. Worship and trust is placed in the God of Abraham, Isaac and Jacob, of Moses and David, of Rahab, Rebekah and Ruth, and

2.

God with Us

God who said, 'Let light shine out of darkness' . . .
has shone in our hearts to give the light of
the knowledge of the glory of God in the face of Jesus Christ.
– 2 Corinthians 4:6

Jesus in Context

Into the history of Israel and the nations comes Jesus the prophet from Nazareth in Galilee. We speak of the New Testament but we must not overlook the deep continuity between the two parts of Scripture. Indeed, many of the writers of the New Testament books are at pains to indicate the one story of God. Jesus does not appear out of the blue. He has a history and must not be cut free from it.

So, for example, Matthew in his gospel sets out the family tree which is full of surprises but traces Jesus back to Abraham (Matt. 1.1–17). Luke goes even further and traces the ancestry of Jesus back to 'son of Adam, son of God' (Luke 3:23–38). Paul is insistent that those who are the followers of Jesus, the first Christians, are children of Abraham and heirs to the great promises of God (Gal. 3:29). John is perhaps the boldest of all the New Testament writers as he introduces his gospel with a grand prologue, speaking of the creative Word in the beginning by which all things came to be, and then announcing that that Word became flesh and lived among us. He is referring to Jesus (John 1:1–14). All through the gospels, Jesus in his ministry clearly uses the language, metaphors and history of God's chosen people. He was, after all, a Jew.

Jesus arrives then into the story of God. He knows of Moses and the great escape from Egypt, of King David, of the humiliation of the years in exile. He would have been told of Daniel and those others who stood against the empires that would engulf Israel and had no honour of God. He would have heard stories of the families who rebelled against the powers of their day and who suffered martyrdom for it. And he is born as the Romans are the great international power with Israel as a captive nation.

At that time there were various responses within Israel to this situation and all play a part in the life of Jesus. So, at one end of the political spectrum, were the appeasers, those who settled to work with the power of the day in compromise. They had family traditions behind them, born to rule as members of the establishment. Such were the Sadducees. At the other end of the spectrum were those who looked for rebellion, prepared to fight and kill in the name of God to establish God's kingdom in the place of foreign gentile rule. Such were the Zealots. Jesus mixed and met all those in this political range, some are even to be found among his disciples. The context of Jesus' birth was seriously political.

We need to remember that this was not politics as separate from religion as we draw such distinctions in our day. In the ancient story of Israel, whoever had political or military power in the world always was answerable to God. To separate religion and politics was unthinkable. There might be a question about who was in power but there never was a question about who reigns! Unlike our modern assumptions this view of the Bible is thoroughly theological. As we saw in the last chapter, life is lived before God. This is the real world. We often experience life as somewhat fragmented but all life is lived before God in whom all things exist. All things come together in the purposes of God and are brought to completion in Christ (Col. 1:17). We may dismiss this thinking as 'medieval' but it was held by some with profound conviction, definitely a positive feature of Christendom.

Beginning the Ministry

One further expression of the continuity between old and new is in Jesus' cousin, John the Baptizer. Again, in their various ways the gospel writers tell of his ministry which they see as one of preparation. He is the promised voice in the wilderness, calling people to get ready for the new thing God was going to do (Isa. 40:3–5; Matt. 3:1–11; Mark 1:2–8; Luke 3:1–20). His message was direct, 'Repent, for the kingdom of heaven has come near' (Matt. 3.2).[1] This is startling news for a people who looked and longed for God's promises to be fulfilled, for the coming of Messiah.[2] The call to repent did not only mean expressing sorrow for the past but also involved turning in a new direction, living differently, and John's token of this was baptism, for both Jews and Gentiles. His was a new movement with a very old history. Among those who came for baptism was the carpenter from Nazareth. John is initially thrown by Jesus' request but is persuaded as Jesus insists on following all that God requires in solidarity with God's claim on Israel and the nations (Matt. 3:15). Jesus identifies himself with John's ministry announcing the new thing God is about to do. The gospel writers all link Jesus' baptism with the Holy Spirit and the affirmation of Jesus' relationship to the Father, a theme we shall return to in the next chapter.

From the first, Jesus knew times of testing and temptation (Mark 1:12–13; Matt. 4:1–11; Luke 4:1–13). What kind of a struggle was this for Jesus? It could be read as a story of Jesus working out what it meant for him to fulfil his calling as Son of God with the power that came with such a calling. But in the context of the gospel setting there is a conflict even here with the empire. Who does rule the world, and how does that rule find expression?

As John's ministry is completed, in fact as he is arrested, Jesus strides on stage, preaching, 'The time is fulfilled, and the kingdom of God has come near; repent, and believe in the good news' (Mark 1:15). We have already noted the religious/political meaning of the world 'kingdom'. It is a loaded term and scholars often argue that it is best translated as 'reign' or 'rule' to emphasize the active nature of the term. God reigns now! The full meaning of the rule of God will include the future but there is no doubting the significance of the now in the life and ministry of Jesus. This is the claim that in the life and ministry of Jesus God is at work, the God of the covenant promises, the God of Israel and the nations. The Promised One is here. Early on in his ministry Jesus chose twelve disciples to be with him, twelve for the tribes of the new Israel, another expression of continuity, a new phase in the ongoing movement of God.

The Kingdom in Conflict

From the first, according to all four gospel writers, Jesus found himself in conflict and there seems to be something intentional about this. Obviously lack of space does not permit any exhaustive list but here are some illustrations of what was going on in the life and ministry of Jesus.

There were issues about what constituted faithful living for those true to God. Jesus did not dismiss the Jewish Torah (teaching) but he took the meaning and implications of it deeper. For example, it was a humane law to teach an eye for and eye and a tooth for a tooth in just recompense for a wrong done, restricting revenge (Exod. 21:34). But Jesus calls for a new form of non-violent response (Matt. 5:38–41).

The stories of Jesus' healing and exorcisms describe some kind of conflict. When confronted by a man with leprosy, Jesus does the extraordinary thing of touching him. Mark says this was an act of pity which would have made Jesus unclean and unacceptable. But a variant reading in Greek even suggests this was done in anger, as if Jesus was deeply affronted by this challenge to the rule of God (Mark 1:41). Sickness, demon possession, all these were faced out by Jesus as he proclaimed the presence of the kingdom (Luke 11:20).

The story of Jesus being tested in the desert after baptism is loaded with conflict imagery (Matt. 4:1–11; Luke 4:1–13). These temptations carry political implications, for example, a compromise with Satan which allows ruling the world. There is the heavy moment at Caesarea Philippi when Peter declares Jesus to be the Christ of God and immediately questions Jesus' teaching about the suffering Christ. As Peter makes his pitch Jesus retorts with vigour, 'Get behind me, Satan!', as Peter offers the old temptation that Jesus will resist (Mark 8:27–33).

Jesus found himself in conflict with popular ideas of being the Christ of God and what that might mean for Israel's future. As John tells the story of Jesus feeding the great multitude (John 6:1–15) the people understandably respond but in an inappropriate way. They want to make him king but they misunderstand the nature of Jesus' reign. So he withdraws by himself. He did not seek fame for its own sake nor was his rule to be based on the popular vote.

Inevitably there were arguments and disagreements as to what was the best response to the Roman presence and demands on Israel. Those Jewish teachers who disliked and distrusted Jesus set traps for him to get him into trouble with either the people or the Romans. So there was the incident with the coin and the question of whether taxes should be paid to Rome (Mark 12:13–17; Luke 20:20–26). Which of the various Jewish groups will Jesus side with in his response? Jesus will not play this game but offers an enigmatic politically acute answer.

And so the list could go on. Jesus was a disturbing figure in many ways – and remains so. Let's come at this matter again via the way he often called into question many of the assumptions of the faith and politics of the day.

The Disturbing Figure of Jesus

He caused a rumpus in his home town as he read the Scriptures and preached (Luke 4:16–30). Perhaps the congregation were waiting for yet another sermon affirming God's regard for Israel and their special place in God's eye. At first the sermon went well until Jesus used two illustrations of God's compassionate goodness, both of them to foreigners: the widow at Zarephath, and Naaman, the Syrian soldier. The congregation soon had had enough of this and looked to run the preacher out of town. But Jesus often called into question any exclusive notions of God. He taught that God sends the rain on the just and the unjust; he causes the sun to rise on his enemies and his friends and God's children should live this way (Matt. 5:43–8).

Jesus challenged assumptions about the nature of the successful life and of being a great person. Great people throw their weight around and keep others in their place (Mark 10:43–5). It is assumed that a successful person owns many possessions because wealth is clearly understood to be God's blessing, a view not unknown in some contemporary forms of church life. Jesus knew that both

God and money were demanding taskmasters but he was quite clear no one could serve them both (Matt. 6:24). A choice had to be made. Was life to be lived before God or not? And as for being a great leader, Jesus taught that neither his way, nor that of his disciples, was to be the way of making others feel the weight of your supposed authority. Those who are great in Jesus' way give service, give themselves (Mark 10:41–5). One of the most remarkable pictures of Jesus in the whole gospel story is of him on his knees washing the feet of his disciples (John 13:1–20). If Jesus is to be spoken of as a king then he is clearly unlike any other king the world has known.

And then there's the family. It would be wrong to suggest that Jesus did not care too much about family life and relationships. After all, one of his last words was of compassion for his mother Mary and his entrusting her to the care of a disciple (John 19:25–7). Why should anyone question Jesus' valuing of this crucial form of relationships? Because on several occasions Jesus questions the absolute hold a narrow view of family relations can have on people's lives and says only God has that absolute claim. On one occasion Jesus' family members are asking for him but he responds by asking just who are his family. He asserts that in the way of God's rule those who do God's will are family (Mark 3:31–5). Can it be that there are relationships thicker than blood in God's new creation? Jesus challenges assumptions about family, nationhood, race and gender.

Again, the list could go on and on as Jesus' life before God is recalled. Jesus was a controversial figure. He was the bearer of God's *shalom* but he told his disciples that this peace is not like the world's peace (John 14:27). He told them bluntly that to follow him would mean persecution, rejection and even death (Mark 8:34 – 9:1). His understanding of the ways of God meant a challenge to many of the assumptions of the world. He seems contradictory to many of our ways now when he seeks to forgive, to have compassion, to turn from violent answers that are no answers, to live in love and love alone. Can this really be the way of God's kingly rule on earth? If it is, then conflict of some kind is essential to the story. Recall for a moment Jesus' insistence on going to Jerusalem, how he set his face resolutely and how he told his disciples what it would mean (e.g. Mark 10:33). It seems that in the context of Jesus' ministry such tensions are real and go with a life of faithfulness before God. Perhaps we should have noticed that from the very beginning, when soon after his birth he had to be on the run as a refugee from a local dictator set on removing all possible competitors (Matt. 2:13–23). As we will see, attempts to frustrate God's purposes are relatively regular features of the story of life before God.

The Jewish and Roman leaders of the time seem to have found Jesus disturbing, an unwelcome, potentially unsettling presence among the people. Any careful reading of the Gospels conveys a sense of impending crisis. Jesus at the last enters the city of Jerusalem.[3] He comes publicly to the centre. His arrival is heavy with symbolism, of one who comes to rule in peace, riding not on a stallion but on a donkey. It is hard to escape the provocative nature of this action. His activity in the temple is extraordinary and, if he were not a marked man before, he certainly would be after causing such chaos. He asserts that his response has to do with the corrupt and sinful use made of this building intended as a house of prayer for all nations (Matt. 21:12–17; Mark 11:1–11; Luke 19:45–8). John tells this story early in his gospel (John 2:13–25). Does he do that to make a theological point about Jesus?

Removing This Dangerous Man

After such a public act there are plots by the authorities to kill Jesus. All the gospel writers, and Paul, understand that those in governance see Jesus as a political disturber, a troublemaker, a threat. We might ask why his present-day disciples are seen as good quiet citizens. We ask for Jesus to bring peace to our souls but what if he brings not peace but a sword, albeit for non-coercive, non-violent purposes (Matt. 10:34)? Again we ask, how does this life look before God?

In the end, they get him, Caiaphas and Pilate between them. John's picture of Jesus before Pilate is very dramatic as issues of truth and sovereignty are raised (John 18:28–38). Jesus suffers at the hands of those in power, a cruelty born out of envy, fear, pride and closed-mindedness. He is given to the soldiers who beat him up, scourge him and humiliate him. He is taken outside the city and killed in the way Romans deal with troublemakers and terrorists. Jesus is crucified, dead and buried. It seems at first that here is yet another idealist ground to nothing under the wheels of powerful machines. Just who is it that runs the world?

The testimony of Israel's faith shared by Jesus is, quite simply, that God rules. But there is no doubt that the followers of Jesus were broken people, broken with despair at the cross. They had had such hopes of Jesus, bearer of the kingdom. Until, after Friday, they came to the third day. The way they tell the story underlines honestly the fact that no one expected to find anything but a corpse to clean and leave for dead. That is why only the women come to the grave – but they find the tomb is empty! They receive the message which the disciples are going to find hard to believe that Jesus the Christ is risen, raised by God from the dead. It is totally unexpected. They are surprised by God!

It is Jesus of the scars and wounds who is raised, Jesus the crucified, who gave his life, who did not spit back, who prayed for those who were crucifying him, who taught and lived the way of love to the end, a way which called into question all the assumptions of those in power. This Jesus God raised! It is not over those who assumed political or religious authority and power that God spoke the great 'Yes' of resurrection. It is this Jesus, the Christ. He is the Christ not in spite of suffering and sacrifice but because of it. The early Christians found new insights into those earlier texts about a suffering servant of the Lord. God was remaining faithful to the ancient promises by doing a new thing.

Incarnation and New Creation

So what was happening in this Jesus? The first and subsequent disciples found themselves thinking about this man. Who is this Christ whose life was marked by the unexpected, calling so many assumptions into question about God and Israel's story? What are we to say about him? When they wrote up their memories in proclamation, the disciples were quick to affirm the depth of relationship Jesus had with the One he called Father. All those hours he spent alone in prayer; all that struggle that went on in the garden, was that the final test as to whether he would trust God until the end or not? What was the relationship between God and Jesus? They found they had to ask such questions because the truth was that they discovered they could not think of Jesus without thinking of God and they could not think of God without thinking of Jesus.

Jesus had somehow become part of the very idea of God. It wouldn't do to say, simply, that Jesus was last and best of the prophets, an extremely good and faithful man. It would not do to say that God was out of the picture in the life of Jesus, as it were, until coming to rescue him at resurrection. They found they had to say things like, 'In Christ God was reconciling the world to himself' (2 Cor. 5.19). They said that the Word that was at the beginning, by whom all things were made, became flesh and lived among us (John 1.1–14). They were struggling with language, trying to say that Jesus was both and inseparably God for us and human for us.

Jesus, they came to believe, was God among us, God with us as never before in flesh. Jesus was the revelation of God, in the things he taught and the deeds he performed. In his weakness of service, washing feet, this was God among us. In his seeming powerlessness before Pilate and the soldiers, this was God among us. In his life of service, sacrifice and love, this was God among us. In his words and deeds of forgiveness, in his giving of himself on the cross into the hands of God, this was God among us.

The language is being stretched to the limit, of course. Finding the appropriate way to talk of Jesus became and remains a major issue for Christians. A whole branch of theology called Christology developed which engaged huge important arguments about the right way to speak of Jesus and God. It is not our purpose here to give any account of that now, only to recognize that it happened, that there were issues of understanding the relationship between the prophet from Nazareth in Galilee and the God of Israel. Could it really be the case that in Jesus God was, as it were, opening the divine heart to the world and that the promised new creation was beginning in him?

Particularly striking is the fact that the first disciples, almost all of them Jewish by upbringing and therefore monotheists by conviction, started to call Jesus risen from the dead 'the Lord'. They came to believe that from first to last, from Bethlehem to

Golgotha and the empty tomb this had been the work of God. But it would not do to suggest that God had somehow used this man Jesus, taken him over as it were. They used the language of Father and Son to express the intensity of relationship as Jesus had done. But then Jesus had also said, 'The Father and I are one' (John 10:30). Did he mean one in moral sense and purpose, or was there a deeper sense of one in being? And what of those great 'I am' sayings when Jesus took to himself that affirmation that was the holy name of God (e.g. Exod. 3:13–15; John 6:35,41,48,51; 8:12,58; 11:25)?

Eventually, later disciples were to use the word 'incarnation'. Jesus was God in human flesh. That was the only way they could express what had happened among them. It was not enough to say that Jesus was special in the way that Moses, David, Isaiah, Esther or Hannah were special partners with God in God's purposes. Jesus was unique in the divine partnership, being at the same time God and human. What other philosophies and religions held resolutely separate the disciples found inseparably united. The Word became flesh – God incarnate – and these were terms used about Jesus and him alone.

The Ascended Lord

There was one further matter. Following the stories of Jesus appearing to the disciples after the resurrection comes the ascension. In John's gospel it all seems to happen in one great movement; Jesus goes to the cross, to death, to glory, to the Father, ascended, giving the Spirit (John 20:1–23). It is Luke among the gospel writers who tells the story of events spaced out in time: empty tomb, resurrection appearances, ascension, Pentecost. The language of ascension seems strange to our modern ears but one thing we must not overlook is the fact that this is the biblical language of power and authority. This is directly illustrated in the letter to the Ephesians 1:17–23. For the purposes of this chapter we cannot fail to notice the political implications of this affirmation. The ascension is surely among the most politically significant doctrines of the New Testament. Jesus is Lord, raised to the place of honour, authority and power. This God has declared, and all other claimants to authority over us are at best relative to the claim of Jesus Christ, the one to whom all authority in heaven and on earth has been given (Matt. 28:18).

Who is this Christ? Whatever later emperors, monarchs, religious leaders or ordinary disciples may have made of him, the New Testament is clear that Jesus is the Christ and the Christ is Jesus. He is God's own self-revelation. There is more to God than Jesus, as it were, but certainly not less when it comes to discerning the nature and ways of God. The doctrine of the incarnation has huge implications for faith in God. We list some of them but not in any order of priority or necessity.

There is the mark of humility about Jesus from the very beginning. He was born in strange uncomfortable circumstances, because of the desires and demands of others. He did not seek possessions and at his death had only the clothes on his back. There was no place for him to lay his head, not even at death. He was a humble man who did not live for himself. He said that you cannot serve God and money (Matt. 6:24).

His ministry involved the invitation of others but never coercion. He did not threaten those who opposed him. At one point when the early disciples were concerned because the great crowds seemed to be slipping away Jesus imply said they could go too if they wished (John 6:67). He did not seek to control the lives of other people. He spent a lot of his time with marginalized, even problematic, people. He could be found with tax collectors (usually disliked because they served the Romans), with sinners (those who did not take the law of God with the seriousness others required), with women, children, diseased and otherwise disregarded people. His sharing meals with such as these is a notable part of the story of the Christ. He had a positive response to those assumed to be the nation's enemies. There is the remarkable story of his conversation with a Samaritan women (John 4:1–42). He was not above entering the home of Roman soldiers in order to heal their children and servants. He did not think that the public acts of religious duty were themselves the heart of the matter. So he was in trouble with those who surrounded the Sabbath with laws which were more important to them than human healing and justice. He could be withering in his comments about religious hypocrisy, a matter of play-acting and not the real thing at all (Matt. 23).

He taught in parables, a way of engaging his listeners in the search for meaning and truthful practice. He was not dogmatic and insistent upon what had to be believed, as if that was what trusting God was all about. His leadership of the twelve was never in doubt but it was a leadership of service and example, not the pulling of rank. So, he washed his disciples' feet and, in this action and others, set them an example not so much to copy as to follow.

He lived to serve and love the Father God whatever his personal wishes might be. There is no place where this is more evident than in the Garden of Gethsemane where Jesus admits to the Father his desire to have some other way than suffering and death before him. But if it is what God wants (Mark 14:32–6) . . . He did not think equality with God was something to be grasped or exploited. When people called him 'good', or asked him about what was good he told them that only God was good (Luke 18:19). He sought the glory of God, not human praise.

He often found himself in controversy because of his teaching and practice of the kingdom of God. He did not hide or run from this fact. He never oppressed others. He responded to people with compassion not with condemnation. He refused to share the easy righteousness of the majority. He would not condemn the woman found in adultery and neither would he condone her (John 7:53 – 8:11). He looked on people with compassion. He was not judgemental. He worked with his disciples, however frail and misunderstanding of him they might be. He had called them and was committed to them, like God in covenant love. His was a ministry of partnership, never a one-man band. The power that was in him was for others and not for his own use or self-advancement. When people began to get overexcited about his miracles he soon sought to withdraw from their praise.

He is the Christ of the cross. In his flesh and blood he was crucified, killed and buried. People did this to him but there is an important sense that he gave up his life rather than seek to save it by methods he rejected. Whenever Jesus was attacked because of the claims of the kingdom of God he taught, he did not fight back.

In summary, Jesus the Christ was in many ways faithful to the religion in which he came. He went to temple with his parents. He attended synagogue. But he was also a dissenter, at least as far as some of the ways of practising the faith were concerned.

He challenged the theology and the practices of his day. We could go on for this list is far from exhaustive. What it does begin to do is set out a description that Jesus is the Christ and the Christ is Jesus. He provides the most important criteria for what it means to serve and live in the name of God. It is Jesus Christ who sets out the fullest revelation of God the world has yet received. We shall have every reason to keep returning to his story and those of his early followers.

The Fullest Revelation of God

The story may be read in such a way that it gives the impression that Jesus lived under the requirements of Roman authority without too much discomfort. But the fact is that there are moments of conflict for Jesus from the moment of his birth. Certainly many of his early followers urged one another to be good citizens, honouring authority, paying taxes, submitting to those whom they assumed God was using for government (e.g. Paul in Rom. 13:1–7 and Peter in 1 Pet. 2:13–17). But it was this Roman Empire that crucified Jesus. The ambiguity we found earlier in the previous chapter is here also. How do Christ and any faithful disciples relate to the political realities of the day, then and now? And how can we be sure it is the Christ revealed in Jesus who is being followed and not the assumptions of the society we share? Later disciples of Jesus thought hard about just who Jesus was and set about trying to express the great claims theologically. We shall come to these later. However, to end this chapter, we offer three illustrations of how the story of Jesus has been worked out in particular situations.

The first of these is the vociferous denunciation of the institution of slavery by the youngest of the Cappadocian Fathers (so-called because they came from Cappadocia which is now modern Turkey) Gregory of Nyssa (c.335–95). In order to fully appreciate the force of Gregory's condemnation it is important to note that Constantine himself passed laws designed to improve the conditions of slaves, such as keeping families together, as well as laws that enabled slaves to be freed, for example by enabling someone claimed by another as a slave to have the opportunity to find a third party that would vouch for their free status.[4] While this certainly casts a softer light on Constantine,[5] who is so often merely vilified as a great corruptor of the church, Gregory's condemnation of the institution of slavery itself goes much further:

> I got me slaves and slave-girls (Ecc. 2:7). For what price, tell me? What did you find in existence worth as much as this human nature? What price did you put on rationality? How many idols did you reckon the equivalent of the likeness of God? . . . *God said, let us make man in our own image and likeness* (Gen. 1:26). If he is in the likeness of God, and rules the whole earth, and has been granted authority over everything on earth from God, who is his buyer, tell me? Who is his seller? To God alone belongs this power; or rather, not even to God himself. For *his gracious gifts*, it says, *are irrevocable* (Rom. 11:29). God would not therefore reduce the human race to slavery, since he himself, when we had been enslaved to sin, spontaneously recalled us to freedom. But if God does not enslave what is free, who is he that sets his own power above God's?[6]

For Gregory, then, the institution of slavery itself is incompatible with the gospel precisely because it resists God's saving purpose by attempting to divide and master what God has united in Jesus Christ. Gregory reads the text of Ecclesiastes through the lens of the *imago Dei* and if it is the case that Christ has indeed entered into history there is no longer any time or space for unjust arrangements of the social and political order. The restoration of humanity, that is, our redemption, is not an abstract promise but a concrete practice, a body that is enacted in our participation in the purposes of God.

A second illustration of the conflict Christ can bring comes from that time in England's history when King Henry VIII needed but found difficulty in producing a male heir. Reformation was abroad in much of Europe and there were those in England asking sharp questions about what it was to be the true church. Henry, for a variety of reasons, was ready to establish the Church of England over which he might reign without the restrictions of a foreign pope. It is hard at times to distinguish genuine religious convictions from political necessities of power. However, the Church of England came into being with its own powerful bishops appointed by the king, with its own book of services and prayers which were to be used, along with a new authorized translation of the Bible to be read in the churches.

There were some people for whom this 'reformation' did not go nearly far enough. They sensed that England had exchanged one form of religious control for another. Some of them felt this so strongly that they left the country and went to Holland where there was greater religious freedom. One who made this journey was Thomas Helwys. In Amsterdam he met with others who had travelled farther down the reformation road, even to the point of pressing the question where the true church was to be found and, in consequence, asking about what it was to join the church and be baptized. Helwys and some others with him were baptized as believers and so formed an early Baptist congregation. But Helwys believed you could not witness to England from Holland so he came home in 1611 and established the first English Baptist church on English land, at Spitalfields near London.

He brought with him the manuscript of a book he had written under the title, *A Short Declaration of the Mystery of Iniquity*.[7] He is strong in his affirmation that Jesus Christ is Lord and he draws out one very direct implication. Remember we are in a Christendom situation where the monarch is head of the church and Parliament decides on how the church shall be governed and worship. In a hand-written note to King James I he bluntly asserts that the king is a mortal man and not God and has no power over the immortal souls of his subjects. In the book he argues that in national affairs the king has the right to call for the obedience of the people. But then, boldly, he says that this authority does not extend to matters of faith and religion. In a very early plea for religious liberty Helwys writes, 'For men's religion to God is between God and themselves. The king shall not answer for it. Neither may the king be judge between God and man. Let them be heretics, Turks, Jews, or whatsoever, it appertains not to the earthly power to punish them in the least measure.'[8] The content of the book makes it clear that Helwys' argument is not the modern one of human rights and the freedom of religion but one that is strictly christological. Since Christ reigns the king's rule is under the rule of Christ. Christ has come to set us free from these human tyrannies. Here Christ is potentially in conflict with the claims of the monarch and Parliament. The monarch is accountable to God. He cannot usurp the divine prerogative. Helwys took a bold stand for which he suffered.

A third illustration involves Adolf Hitler who had, for the most part, come legitimately to power, elected by the people of Germany. Many Germans looked to a strong leader to make their country great again. But soon things began to happen that disturbed some Christians. The attitude taken to the Jewish people, enforced in laws which caused them to suffer, was one of these issues. For many Christians, loyalty to Hitler as head of state was unquestioned. They were Lutherans who had a long tradition of understanding God ruling the world through the two ways of his word and the duly appointed government. They became known as the *Deutsche Christen*, the German Christians, those who supported Hitler and his policies.

But there were other Christians who found their understanding of their vocation in Christ to be at odds with the way of the nation and its national church. Some of them came together and made a confession of their faith at a town called Barmen, which became known as the Barmen Declaration:

> 'I am the way, and the truth, and the life; no one comes to the Father, but by me' (John 14:6).
> 'Truly, truly I say to you, he who does not enter the sheepfold by the door, but climbs in by another way, that man is a thief and a robber . . . I am the door; if anyone enters by me, he will be saved' (John 10:1, 9). Jesus Christ, as he is attested to us in Holy Scripture, is the one Word of God whom we have to hear, and which we have to trust and obey in life and death.
> We reject the false doctrine, that the church could and should recognize as a source of its proclamation, beyond and besides this one Word of God, yet other events, and powers, historic figures and truths as God's revelation.[9]

This radically Christocentric affirmation was the basis on which many 'Confessing Church' pastors found they were in conflict with official national policies. The compulsion in religion, the terrible wrongs done to the Jews, the threat to the liberty of the church to preach the gospel, all this and more meant a small but significant minority of Christians in Germany found themselves against the government. Again, this was not because of political differences so much as convictions about Jesus Christ. Among those who became leaders in the Confessing Church and suffered for it were Karl Barth, Martin Niemöller and Dietrich Bonhoeffer. As far as they were concerned, the German state had gone too far. The Christ was not Jesus Christ but a saviour of their national desire and making, a very different God fashioned in their own image. They were faced with the difficult issue of how to be a good citizen and a faithful Christian, faithful that is to Christ Jesus.

3.

God the Spirit

> If the Spirit of him who raised Jesus from the dead
> dwells in you, he who raised Christ from the dead
> will give life to your mortal bodies also through
> his Spirit that dwells in you.
>
> – Romans 8:11

The Powerful Metaphor of Spirit

What has become obvious in the previous two chapters is that there is no systematic elucidation of name 'God' in the Bible. The name is rich in meaning. We have discerned creator and sustainer, we have noted different aspects of sovereignty, and been struck by the absence of abstractions but rather an emphasis on the particular in history. We are offered different pictures of God in the story and just when we think we have found the answer to our search for definition we find ourselves set off in another direction. Is it ever possible to give expression to the meaning of God in words? There seems to be something fundamentally elusive about God in the Bible.

This recognition seems to even more obvious when we explore another set of biblical words, metaphors, gathered around the important word 'Spirit'. 'God is spirit', says Jesus in the theologically loaded conversation with a woman from Samaria, 'and those who worship him must worship in spirit and truth' (John 4:24). Spirit is clearly a key term.

When we come again to the Bible, however, we find an abundance of ways of speaking of Spirit. Metaphors tumble over one another. Spirit is pictured, among other ways, as wind, both as gentle breeze and as overpowering storm; or as fire, as living water, as breath. Immediately we notice all these have a dynamic quality about them, disturbing and creative. Sometimes the Spirit is pictured as a bird but always one that is uncaged and free.

So, if we are to make another quick and admittedly superficial journey through the Bible story we discover the Spirit there at the beginning, moving on the face of the waters (Gen. 1:2). The Hebrew word ruach, meaning spirit or wind, is there at the beginning of God's creative and sustaining work, life-giving, bringing order out of chaos, turning ugliness into beauty. We read of Bezalel, chief architect of the tabernacle, who was filled with the spirit of God to produce all manner of things beautiful in his work (Exod. 31:1–3). Judges and leaders, prophets and teachers are all raised up by God as the Spirit comes upon them. Thus Spirit is not some private possession or achievement but is a gift. Spirit is the activity of God.

Sometimes this work seems angular, from the margins, sharp and judging. So there are the stories of Nathan rebuking David and Elijah confronting Ahab. The Spirit's work is to speak by the prophets, speaking truth to power, confronting and rebuking the monarchs who have overstepped the mark before God. This is the enabling Spirit that can come upon men and women for the purposes of God. Thus Gideon (Judg. 6:34) and Samson (Judg. 14:6) knew moments of inspiration and empowerment for God's work of liberation. Victories are won 'Not by might, nor by power, but by my spirit, says the LORD of hosts' (Zech. 4:6).

There is also the closest connection between God as active Spirit and the human spirit. It is God's breath that is breathed into the dust bringing the living to be. Human spirits (persons) can be troubled by God, overcome by God, and have God withdraw the Spirit from them. Thus Spirit is the source of physical life, the source of wisdom and knowledge, the capacity to undertake and do the will of God. This is always and only a temporary endowment, not a personal possession. It is the active work of God in partnership, God and humankind united in Spirit.

The Spirit and Jesus

It comes as no surprise to find the Spirit of God, the Holy Spirit, fundamental to the life and ministry of Jesus. Mary conceives by the Holy Spirit (Matt. 1:18). In a dream (the work of the Spirit?), Joseph is warned about Herod's intentions and so the family become refugees in Egypt. A feature of John the Baptizer's prophetic ministry is to alert the people to one who will come and baptize with the spirit and fire (Matt. 3:11). And when Jesus is baptized by John, God is active in the Spirit, like a dove alighting on Jesus (Matt. 3:16). This is no partial and occasional visit – the Spirit abides in and with Jesus. Significantly, it is the Spirit who leads Jesus (Mark has 'drives' Jesus) into the wilderness for a time of testing. When Jesus begins his public ministry 'filled with the power of the Spirit' (Luke 4:14), he comes to his home town and reads from Isaiah the prophet a passage speaking of one on whom the Spirit of the Lord has come for the work of liberation. 'Today', Jesus declares to the congregation, 'this scripture has been fulfilled' (Luke 4:16–21). Jesus' ministry is a full expression of the activity of God, the work of the Spirit.

In John's Gospel we are given some serious teaching and reflection on the Spirit (John 14 – 17). We have already heard Jesus speak with Nicodemus about the importance of water and the Spirit, of being born from above, of God (John 3:1–8), but it is in the upper-room discourses that we are led to some of the fullest teaching about the Spirit in the New Testament: 'If you love me, you will keep my commandments. And I will ask the Father, and he will give you another Advocate, to be with you for ever. This is the Spirit of truth, whom the world cannot receive, because it neither sees him nor knows him. You know him, because he abides with you, and he will be in you' (John 14:15–17).

The Spirit and Disciples

We note that the Spirit is identified as another Advocate or Paraclete. Who is the first Advocate? It is Jesus who now asks this gift for the disciples. The key to understanding the work of

God the Spirit is Jesus. The Spirit will not be only in the disciples but will remain with them, be alongside them, as strength-giver (comforter), teacher, advocate, intercessor. To put the point sharply, the Spirit will be to the disciples what Jesus has been, God among and in them.

The Spirit will guide the disciples into all truth. But Jesus is the way, the life and the truth (John 14:6) so the connection between the Spirit and Jesus is affirmed again. It is by the work of the Spirit that the disciples will be able to call to mind all that they were taught by Jesus. By the Spirit they will understand his life and teaching in the coming time when he is no longer with them. In the Fourth Gospel, truth is something to be lived and done, not just a proposition to be understood and believed. Thus living in the truth, in the Spirit, is not to be separated from discipleship, from keeping God's commandments.

However, the world will find this an alien spirit. The world cannot receive him, it neither sees nor knows him. So there will be conflict, tension, persecution as the Spirit underlines the judgement of the ruler of this present age (John 16:7–11).

There is an anonymity about the Spirit in the sense that the Spirit's task is to point to Jesus, to call his teaching to mind. The Spirit takes of the things of Christ and shows them to us. The Spirit does not seek to draw attention to himself (John 16:13–15).

The Gospel of John ends at some speed. John is not above the relocating of events in order to make a theological point.[1] Certainly he wants to hold together what is often separated in the Christian calendar. So we move quickly in John from crucifixion to burial, to resurrection, ascension, to gift of the Spirit all on the same day, as if it were one complete action of God, which it is. Is John offering us a different reflection on 'time'? All through his gospel he seems to see things differently, as the action of God. It is Luke who gives more space and takes us through resurrection, ascension, and gift of the Spirit with days between. It is Luke's way of telling the story that has shaped the calendar and worship of the church, for which we might be thankful for these, along with Christmas, are the great festivals of the faith. Luke's way of telling the story is there in the way school terms reflect the story of God in the Christian year.

The Acts of the Spirit

With Luke we pick up the frightened disciples of Jesus in Jerusalem. They are witnesses to the resurrection and ascension of Jesus. They have heard his promise of the gift of the Holy Spirit. They have been told to wait. It was on the Jewish feast of Pentecost that it happened. The Spirit came as wind and fire, multiple languages and a new boldness to overcome any fears (Acts 2). The promise was kept. The Spirit was given. Luke's second volume is usually called 'The Acts of the Apostles', but we would not be first to suggest the alternative title 'The Acts of the Holy Spirit'. We are given not a theological treatise on the Spirit so much as the story of those who received the Spirit as the gift of the Father as Jesus promised in prayer (John 14:16). The frightened disciples became bold witnesses to what God had done in Jesus, his death and resurrection. It was not long before they were in trouble with the authorities, facing the powers of the day, up before the courts. But they spoke openly and boldly and soon prison, rejection and even martyrdom came their way. But they were positive about one great conviction, namely that they must obey God rather than any human authority (Acts 4:19–20; 5:29). Something new had happened in the life of this small company of disciples. It was not just that they were convinced of the resurrection of Jesus and knew his presence with them. It was this gift of God, the activity of God, the Spirit of God in them and among them. By the Spirit they were caught up into the new thing God was about in and through Jesus.

It is never the purpose of this book to give an exhaustive account of the doctrine of God, as has become obvious to the reader. But we are setting out a doctrine, technically called pneumatology, the story of one and the same Spirit. So here are some aspects of the Spirit in Acts and the epistles.

Conflict Again

We do not have to read far into the Acts of the Apostles before we find the apostles in conflict with the authorities because of their proclamation of Jesus. A crippled beggar is healed at the temple, causing the amazement which followed the works of healing done by Jesus. This man is healed in the name of Jesus of Nazareth (Acts 3:1–10). The crowd gathers and Peter preaches to them. His message is what God has done in Jesus, the one raised from the dead. Before long the authorities appear and Peter and John are in prison, although many listeners believed the message. The next day leads to an enquiry by the priestly authorities. Their concern is by what power or in what name this work has been done. Peter, 'filled with the Holy Spirit' (Acts 4:8), again speaks of Jesus and God's work of salvation. The authorities try to silence him, warning Peter and John that they may no longer speak or teach in the name of Jesus, but Peter tells them this is impossible. Rather like Jeremiah (Jer. 20:9) they must speak the message they are given. The end result is that the apostles were often in trouble, brought before the courts, but Peter summed up their response to the persistent call for them to desist from speaking of Jesus in the affirmation that they 'must obey God rather than any human authority' (Acts 5:29). This is the Spirit that is found in the prophets, those called to speak God's word to those in power.

God's empowering of some to confront the (mis)leaders of the day is a big theme in the Bible story as we have already noticed. Those caught up into these conflicts are not independent radically minded individuals who might be dismissed as political activists. The way we have come to read the Bible through individualistic spectacles has become a problem for us. It has led to distortions and lack of discernment of God's ways with us together, as servants of God, empowered and inspired by God the Spirit to bear witness to the truth. We are not surprised then when in the story of the early church we are confronted by persecution and martyrdom. Stephen is among those who persist in telling the story of what God has done in Jesus only to be arrested. Luke gives us a full account of the apostle's response, his retelling of the story of God's ways with Israel coming to a climax in Jesus and charging the people with opposing the Holy Spirit (Acts 6:8 – 7:53). In response they stone Stephen to death. He dies with the words of Jesus on his lips, in the power of the Spirit. He witnesses to the last, praying like Jesus for those who kill him (Acts 7:54 – 8:1). Saul of Tarsus saw it happen.

Again we find as a feature of the story of God that those faithful to God, like Jesus, can be in conflict with the powers, authorities and assumptions of their day. They do not set out to make trouble but they are part of a struggle between the ways of God and the will of humankind, finding themselves in situations where the reality of the rule of God breaks through. Who rules? Who is the authority to be obeyed? The Spirit calls and enables not just individuals but the community gathered in the name of Jesus to resist false claims to governance and be faithful to the ways of God. These ways are non-coercive and non-violent and we can discern a line drawn from the witness and ministry of the prophets, from Moses onwards, through Jesus, now appearing in the early church. It is the work of God the Spirit. One aspect of the Spirit's work seems to be this challenging of the status quo especially when it claims the authority and place of God. The Acts of the Apostles and the ongoing story of the church declares that when the reign of God is affirmed in the lives of disciples then that determines the reality of life whatever we assume is the status quo.

Marks of the New People

There is another line of consistency we must note. Earlier we found in the story of God the calling of Abraham and Sarah and the promise to work with them to establish a new people for the sake of all people. We have recalled how Jesus called disciples to be with him and told them that whatever the way of leaders was in their experience it was not to be so among them. They were to be different because they lived the life the kingdom of God. Now in the Acts of the Apostles and the epistles we find the early Christians, the church, a new community with some surprising characteristics. This is the work of the Spirit and here we note three factors in particular.

First, we focus on a story that Luke thought so important that he told it twice in the Acts of the Apostles (Acts 10 – 11). We must remember that most of the first disciples were Jews by religious conviction and upbringing. True enough, Jesus had encounters with Samaritans, told a story with one of them as the hero and seems to have responded to Roman soldiers with respect and compassion. But the context of the early church was one where the division between Jew and Gentile was sharp and deep and the faithful kept clear of the unclean. The story of the experience of Cornelius, a Roman centurion, and Peter the apostle is remarkable, not least because of what happens to them both is something of a surprise. God the Spirit communicates with both of them as God guides the church into new ways. Cornelius, in a vision of an angel, receives a message to send for Peter the follower of Jesus who is in Joppa. This Cornelius does, believing this word has come from God. The next day, Peter at prayer also receives a vision. He sees in a sheet all kinds of animals and food. He is told to kill and eat but Peter refuses because some of these animals are unclean according to the tradition of his faith. This encounter happens three times and there is the message: 'What God has made clean, you must not call profane' (Acts 10:15).

All this is very puzzling for Peter until the messengers from Cornelius arrive. The Spirit tells Peter to meet them and go with them without hesitation. So eventually Peter and some other disciples go to Caesarea. Peter reminds Cornelius that Jews and Gentiles are forbidden to associate. But he also says that God has told him not to call anything he has made unclean. Whereupon Cornelius tells him how God spoke to him and called him to send for Peter. Peter again speaks of Jesus and during the sermon the Holy Spirit comes upon all present, Jews and Gentiles. They all speak in tongues and praise God together. Peter asks if, in the light of this work of God, anyone can withhold baptism – that is, membership in the church – from these Gentiles? The answer, surprising even shocking as it may be, is obvious.

All this was reported to the church in Jerusalem. It led to the recognition that God had given life-giving repentance to the Gentiles. The Spirit was being poured out on all flesh by the God who was no respecter of persons because God was the respecter of all persons! This is a breakthrough response of immense consequences. We ought not to imagine it all passed without any doubts, arguments or hiccups. Read the letter of Paul to the Galatians and you get some sense of the passionate feelings that were involved. We all know that deep-seated prejudices and ways are not overthrown easily. Remember the response to Jesus' first sermon at Nazareth when the congregation turned against him at the positive reference to God's goodness to Naaman the Syrian and the Gentile widow of Zarepath to whom Elijah the prophet ministered (Luke

4:16–30). The preacher only just got out alive! These were not, of course, the only references to God's calling of Gentile people in the divine purpose.

The recalling of the ministry and teaching of Jesus in the power of the Spirit led the first Christians to remarkable ways of life and new understandings of God. They realized that the promise was being fulfilled and God was pouring out the Spirit on all flesh, on young and old, men and women, Jew and Gentile (Acts 2:17–21 where the prophet Joel is quoted). The implications of this gift of the eschatological Spirit, a sure sign of God's purposes of salvation, were hard to grasp. Have we really done so now, we wonder? Undergirding these stories is the conviction that God rules and holds all things together in Christ (Col. 1:15–20). The claim of the church is that this is the true story, more comprehensive that other stories we tell, reflecting our individualism and tribalisms. This story is about the healing of all that is.

The Spirit of Unity and Peace

The apostle writes to the church in Ephesus and, recalling their own experience, tells of God pulling down any dividing wall of hostility between Gentiles and Jews, creating a new humanity in Christ Jesus, the one raised from the dead (Eph. 2:11–22). This was a Spirit-inspired challenge to many centuries of division, with even hatred and war. But here was God making peace, uniting what was divided, healing what was broken. It was the new life in Jesus, revealed in the ministry of Jesus in the social and political life of humankind. As we have come to expect, it involves seeing things differently. For example, we make great play of distributing bread for the hungry of the world. We assume that the bread is ours to give but has it not always been theirs? That the world belongs to God, the earth and all its people (Ps. 24:1), is the truth of the matter.

This is so far-reaching that it is obvious that the early disciples did not always draw out all the implications of what was happening among them. Take the extraordinary statement of Paul to the Galatians, 'There is no longer Jew or Greek, there is no longer slave or free, there is no longer male and female; for all of you are one in Christ Jesus' (Gal. 3:28). Here is a challenge to ethnic, religious, economic, gender differences, most of which are still with us. Remember the long sad story of the struggle to outlaw slavery, the thousands who died in that fight and were victims of the evil system. The world is not rid of it yet. And the story of women in the church is a witness to a refusal by some to follow the Spirit. Why are there still black congregations and white congregations in the same town? Why are some congregations easy in their economic luxury while other brothers and sisters starve?

Here we touch on another illustration of this new life of the Spirit. True enough, it was only a working out of God's ancient teaching about neighbour love and care. But was it not remarkable that so early the first Christians found an economic dimension to their faith such that in the church in Jerusalem they shared what they had and no one was left in want (Acts 2:43–7; 4:32–7)? Imagine that, not a needy person among them! We can quickly dismiss this 'early experiment' as it has been called but what we cannot deny is that under the influence of the Spirit calling people to the new life in Christ this economic aspect was immediate and proper. Part of the meaning of the word 'fellowship' (*koinonia*) so associated with the work of the Spirit is 'sharing'. How would we defend our huge economic differences in the church today?

What we have come to call the ecumenical movement is itself an aspect of the Spirit's work. The Spirit's work is one of uniting what is separate, healing divisions, taking down walls. The church as the body of Christ is one body with one head. The necessary aspects of the body may be different but they only have full meaning and existence as one body. Healing the brokenness of the church is a work of the Spirit. We have become used to, even defensive of our denominations, forgetting that these can be a form of idolatry as we fail to live in the truth of the one church. There will be no renewal of the church without the work of the Spirit. And perhaps we have to consider that what we can call secular organizations and policies are also related to the Spirit's vision. We are thinking of what Catholic theology calls the 'common good', expressions of which might be the United Nations organization (one meaning of ecumenical is 'all in one house') or a national health service where human need is the activating factor and health does not depend upon having the necessary wealth to pay for the service. Might these human organizations be some of the ways God seeks to govern the world?

Discerning the Work of the Spirit

A second factor in the work of the Spirit follows on from the fact that the early disciples found themselves with social challenges which were deep and demanding. Who was to decide these issues? One of the developments in the story of the Spirit shows how at first, it seemed, the Spirit was given only to discrete individuals in order to fulfil certain crucial tasks. Thus the Spirit is upon Moses and other prophets for the task of leading, judging and proclaiming. At a time of some crisis Moses was ready to pray: 'Would that all the LORD's people were prophets, and that the LORD would put his spirit on them!' (Num. 11:29). However, the gift of the Spirit at Pentecost is upon all flesh. The Spirit is a gift to the church, in every member for the work of ministry (Eph. 4:12), building up the body of Christ.

So, when the challenge emerges concerning God's giving the Spirit to the Gentiles, a large assembly of the church is gathered, to listen, hear testimony, before making a decision (Acts 15). No one voice dominates, claiming to be alone the channel of revelation and wisdom. There is something democratic about the Spirit, such that when important decisions are made together the church can say, 'It has seemed good to the Holy Spirit and to us . . .' (Acts 15:28). It was another early experience of the church that many would come claiming guidance of the Spirit and that what was needed was the gift of discernment (1 John 4:1). Any individual claims were brought to the assembly because each one present was in their devotion to Christ blessed by the Spirit and capable of discerning the truth. No voice was to be silenced. As with the anonymity of the Spirit we have already mentioned there goes a modesty of those alert to the Spirit. We may have in the Spirit one to lead us into all truth, such is the promise of Jesus, but none of us can claim an absolute apprehension of the Spirit's guidance.

This is a difficult area of living. We have no reason to doubt the good news of the Spirit's guidance. But we do have reason to fear the over-confident leader, the council that claim to speak for God when in fact they are not listening to God. There is no escaping the tension here. Holding it and living with it may be one of the chief ways the Spirit enables us to live as God's people. We applaud one contemporary theologian who has made a very insightful contribution to this. We think of Samuel Wells and his book, *Improvisation: The Drama of Christian Ethics*.[2] He knows the importance of Christian decision-making corporately and individually. He is aware of how difficult this can be and how tempting are the short cuts to a supposed but false certainty. He pictures the church as a theatre company given the task of improvising. The players know the story so far. They are able to discern the good characters from the misleading. But now they must continue the story, by improvisation. By living out and developing the characters, by responding to issues when mistakes have been made and wrong roads walked, they live in the story and continue to tell it, calling others to share the life. We recognize the realism of this model and its confidence in the Spirit's guidance. Could this be the way God deals with us, the God who calls but does not control?

One further feature of Well's approach is that it recognizes the elements of surprise that may go with the story. We have noticed how in the Bible the Spirit keeps challenging and disturbing settled ways. This is after all the Spirit that brings life, who causes dead bones to dance and live (Ezek. 37:1–14). A sign of faithfulness in discipleship is openness to the Spirit, to the God of surprises. We think we are settled, we have 'got it right', that nothing more needs to be done, and then the wind blows. We might even try to prevent it, sensing only an inconvenient draught, but this is God's free Spirit, the Spirit of love and life, the renewing transforming Spirit given to the church and let loose in the world.

That it is easy for the powers that be to try to quench the Spirit is all too obvious in the reading of history. History is, after all, written by those with power and they give the 'official' interpretation of events. But there has always been an underside of history, a minority report, small voices never quite silenced. This can take the form of the lone prophet, speaking a word that contradicts the popular voice, as is the case with Micaiah who suffered for his faithfulness to the word of the Lord (1 Kgs 22:4–28). There is often what John Driver has called 'an alternative history', a record of peoples who have been at the margins of power but witnessing, sometimes in opposition to what the official religion declares to be the ways of God.[3] Driver traces the story from the biblical witness through various groups and movements that knew the persecution of the established order, for example, Francis of Assisi, the Lollards, the Anabaptists, George Fox and the Quakers and, in our own time, the Latin-American base communities. This raises the question as to whether human societies of various forms have an inbuilt tendency that makes it hard to respond to the free life of the Spirit. More than a few disciples who have experienced charismatic renewal have not found a welcoming response. All these and many more arose as renewal groups, opposed by those in power, but by God's grace they lived in the power of the Spirit witnessing to God's renewing work. The powers often pronounced them heretical, unorthodox and therefore wrong but all too often, thank God, they have been shown to be genuine expressions of the untamed Spirit of God. God will not leave himself without witnesses however often the powers that be are ready to grieve the Spirit by attempting to silence the living, given word of life.

The issue of discernment remains. The Spirit was given to keep the followers of Jesus in the truth but this is not always easy. Is this new movement a work of God or not? Gamaliel's response is one full of good sense (Acts 5:34–9) and echoes the biblical approach of 'by their fruits you shall know them' (see John 15:1–11). Just because something new does not fit with the accepted wisdom does not mean it is not of God for as John Robinson, one of the Pilgrim Fathers, put it, 'The Lord had more light and truth yet to break forth out of his holy Word.'[4] This is the recognition that we do not have the final word, which is always with God, and it is a mark of spiritual wisdom to be open to the new thing God may be doing or saying.

Divine, Holy Spirit of God

One last reflection. 'Spirit' is a rich term. It is unfortunate that some old translations read John 4:24 as 'God is a spirit.'[5] Such gave hostage to an old dualism which pictured the creation as both material and spiritual, with many 'spirits', good and bad,

God the Spirit

influencing human life. God is then seen as part of this grouping. This is so much less than the biblical vision where God is Spirit. Spirit is of the essence of God's being, the God who stands behind all creation and history, who became flesh and lived among us. We shall take up more of this theme in the next chapter. But for the moment, we affirm the fundamental nature, the primal potency of Spirit. So, as we have earlier indicated, creation is the work of God the Spirit. God is cosmic spirit, existing at the heart of all that is. This includes us, humankind, who share – whether we recognize it or not – a fundamental relationship with God. This goes some way to explain the longings that can be found in so many descriptions of human life and faith. The Spirit calls to us, draws us on, lures us towards God's future. So Paul speaks of the whole universe groaning, longing for the children of God to be revealed, longing to be set free (Rom. 8:19–25). Pentecost might then be understood as a moment when the invisible became visible, when fundamental divinity lights up the cosmos. God as Spirit is universal and eternal, revealed in each human life and in the whole of creation. Creation is 'graced', full of potential to become what God will make of it when God is 'all in all'. Sometimes, by the work of God the Spirit, we are drawn into the wonder and worship this evokes and the fulfilment of all that is. We can never think in too large a sense of the Spirit, God on the loose, Spirit of life, love and hope.

A key issue for us in this book is the sovereignty of God, God's action in the world. Not everything that happens is the work of God. That is obvious, not the least when the Spirit inspires movements of resistance and we learn that God dissents from what we are doing in the church and the world. John Howard Yoder helpfully suggests that asking: 'What is God doing in the world?' may not be the best question. Rather the issues is: 'How do we discern where and how God is acting in all that which is going on in the world? The answer to this question will not be provided by reading the surface of day-to-day history but by the Spirit-led insight of a discerning community.'[6]

PART TWO:

GOD IN THE LIVING TRADITION

4.

The Triune God

For there are three who bear witness in heaven,
the Father, the Word, and the Holy Spirit,
and these three are one.

And there are three who bear witness on earth,
the Spirit, and the water, and the blood,
and these three are one.

– 1 John 5:7[1]

Gesticulating with Words?

To turn from the biblical narrative itself, with which we have been primarily occupied in the first three chapters, to the doctrine of the Trinity may represent to some a descent into the metaphysical quagmires of early Christian battles with long-dead heretics, all of which could preferably be left in the dustbin of history. Indeed, it is a widely held belief expressed in many churches that the doctrine of the Trinity is an abstract piece of theological complexity that is quite possibly irrelevant to our contemporary situation and, in any case, mostly incomprehensible. This general feeling comes, at least somewhat paradoxically, amidst something of a renaissance of Trinitarian theology that has taken place in the twentieth century. Moreover, this sceptical posture about the doctrine of the Trinity goes well beyond the confines of those who regularly occupy the pews on Sunday mornings and is helpfully summarized by Ludwig Wittgenstein's brief assessment of Karl Barth's understanding of the Trinity: 'Theology which insists on the use of *certain* words and phrases and prohibits others makes nothing clearer. It gesticulates with words, as it were, because it wants to say something and does not know how to express it.'[2]

In a more sympathetic tone, John Howard Yoder sums up the sceptical view of the 'usefulness' of the doctrine of the Trinity in his claim that it 'is a solution to an intellectual difficulty that arises if we accept the statements of the Bible. It is not itself a revealed truth, but the solution to the word problem we get into when we accept revelation in Jesus, the continuance of that revelation in the Holy Spirit, and hold to monotheism at the same time.'[3] While certainly more positive about the doctrine of the Trinity than Wittgenstein, it is clear that Yoder relativizes its importance and relegates its significance to secondary theological matters. Perhaps the most powerful way he does so is by understanding it through a particular reading of the socio-political context of the fourth century:

> If we look back at the politics between 325 and 431, at some of the theologians' methods and motives, at the personal quality of Constantine, or if we ask in what sense he was a Christian when he dictated this dogma, then we have to be dubious about giving this movement any authority. If we call into question the acceptance of Hellenistic thought forms foreign to the way the Bible thinks, which fit with neither the Hebrew mind nor, for that matter, with the modern mind, then again we have to challenge whether the creed does us much good.[4]

It is perhaps here more than anywhere else that the caricatures of Constantine's poisonous embrace of the church, which is portrayed primarily through the narrative of the ascendency of the church from persecuted minority status to a place of privilege within Roman imperial society, must be challenged.[5] This is not to say that Yoder's worries about how the doctrine of the Trinity and the creeds more generally have come to be understood are unfounded. Yoder is rightly concerned with the extent to which doctrine may become a substitute set of intellectual beliefs separated from a life of discipleship. The choice between the Jesus of history and the Jesus of doctrine is a false one, as Yoder himself affirms.[6] However, this temptation is not only or even primarily the result of some opaque notion of 'Christendom' and owes far more to the triumph of Enlightenment individualism, into which we have all unwittingly been indoctrinated. The burden of this chapter, then, will be to show how and why the fundamental story of the Christian life is Trinitarian: all of creation comes from the Father, through the Son, and in the Spirit; and salvation is the process of being incorporated into the Son by the Spirit so that we may be led to the Father.

Doctrine and Development

Before moving on, however, it is necessary to distinguish between doctrine and concept in particular and to say something about the nature of theological development in general. First, a distinction must be drawn between the term 'concept', which is an abstract idea, and 'doctrine', which is a teaching or instruction. Both of these terms have a long and complex history. The term 'concept' can be understood as a kind of abstract universal that contains within it multiple particulars. Helpfully illustrating this, Aristotle suggests that when a child first begins to speak they will call all men father and all women mother and only later be able to distinguish between particular men and women.[7] In contrast to this, doctrine can be understood, as Augustine suggests, rather like a teacher of the alphabet who enables others to read and understand texts.[8] In this way, doctrine functions not as a prescribed set of abstract rules and regulations that must be rigorously adhered to but rather more like a compass in what can often be a disorienting world.

For our purposes, this distinction between concept and doctrine is particularly important because our modern minds are increasingly accustomed to conflating them. That is to say, we are wont to treat doctrine itself as an abstract, static, purely intellectual concept and precisely for this reason worries like Yoder's must be seriously reckoned with. However, what we want to argue in this chapter is that when this important distinction is lost, our helpful concern about the extent to which this now deformed concept of doctrine can and does stand in for a life of discipleship must be met with an equally concerted effort to look again at the two thousand year tradition of Christianity. We are convinced that if we undertake a return to the sources of the Christian tradition, particularly in its vital moments and texts, we will find rich resources that are capable of nourishing, invigorating and rejuvenating a life of discipleship today. By learning to reread the classic texts of the Christian tradition we become better equipped to faithfully read the signs of our own times.

This conviction leads directly to our second prefatory note, which has to do with theological development or, more specifically, with what John Henry Newman calls the development of Christian doctrine. It is perhaps at this point that our insistence in the first three chapters on the primacy and irreducibility of the biblical narrative might be understood as an enthusiastic embrace of the Protestant principle of *sola scriptura*. After all, if we are to truly inhabit the biblical narrative in all its rich particularity is this not rather dramatically at odds with later more philosophically driven abstract doctrinal reflections that reshaped the Christian story by borrowing and adapting ideas from the diverse cultures in which it was moving and growing? What this question seeks to separate, namely the biblical narrative and later developments in Christian doctrine, we wish to hold together and it is here that Newman's notion of development becomes particularly helpful. Ideas that capture our collective imaginations, according to Newman, do not exist in a vacuum but rather in the play of lively minds, that is to say, in the complex interactions of judgement, analysis and debate that comprise the life of a community. Significantly, Newman suggests that whatever the risk of corruption, all truly great ideas must engage the existing state of things out of which they arose in the first place if they are to fully blossom.

> At first no one knows what it is, or what it is worth. It remains perhaps for a time quiescent; it tries, as it were, its limbs, and proves the ground under it, and feels its way. From time to time it makes essays which fail, and are in consequence abandoned. It seems in suspense which way to go; it waivers, and at length strikes out in one definite direction. In time it enters upon strange territory; points of controversy alter their bearing; parties rise and fall around it; dangers and hopes appear in new relation; and old principles reappear under new forms. It changes with them in order to remain the same. In a higher world

it is otherwise, but here below to live is to change, and to be perfect is to have changed often.[9]

Extending Aristotle's metaphor with the help of Newman, we might say that development is analogous to the growth of a child, who will spend at least some time trying to walk without actually managing it and will eventually be able to walk on their own without hand-holding or some other external aid only over time and through their own strength and repeated efforts. Put another way, development is the expansion of the implications and possibilities of doctrine as there is time to formulate these by repeatedly circling around the same idea and looking at it from different angles. This is also why we should not expect the development of doctrine to unfold in only one direction. Despite deep contrasts that may be made between saints as different as Francis of Assisi and Thomas Aquinas, for example, they were both doing the same work albeit in different ways.[10]

If, as Augustine taught, theology should seek 'to instruct, to delight, and to move',[11] it may be appropriate to conceive of theological development along the lines of dramatic improvisation. This possibility has been most fully drawn out by Samuel Wells, who we mentioned earlier. Wells provocatively suggests that the Christian life is one in which members are baptized into a biblical and ecclesial drama within which they are invited to participate by attempting to faithfully improvise new expressions of the beauty, truth and goodness of the scriptural witness.[12] Lest the analogy be misunderstood, Wells is quick to note that the point of improvisation is not to be original, clever or witty but rather depends on the ability to act from habit, from formation in and communal discernment of the narrative of which it is an extension through a particular attentiveness to the work of God in history. This notion of theological development as improvisation is particularly helpful because we can see it at work in the biblical narrative itself, whether in Paul's wrestling with the meaning of the cross and resurrection, in the magnificent meditation on the significance of Jesus in the Gospel of John, or in the struggles recounted in the birth and expansion of the church in the Acts of the Apostles. As Newman suggests, this process of development and change is unceasing and the process of improvisation begun in the story of Scripture itself continues throughout the tradition.

We are convinced, however, that ours is more and more a culture of amnesia in which we are surfeited with shopping and anaesthetized with entertainment and, perhaps even more seriously, a culture that actively avoids digging into the tradition because it is remote, difficult, demanding and, therefore, deemed not especially relevant. We have forgotten the significance of doctrine. In this situation, our ability to faithfully improvise becomes seriously impaired and thus we must find ways of addressing this by reclaiming the tradition as a vital source for discipleship today. With these two prefatory notes in mind, then, we turn to what can be only the briefest of sketches of one of the most vital and creative moments in the Christian tradition, namely the Council of Nicaea and the beginnings of the formulation of the doctrine of the Trinity, about which Augustine rightly notes that 'nowhere is a mistake more dangerous, or the search more laborious, or discovery more advantageous'.[13]

Before and After Nicaea

The most obvious point of departure for a rudimentary understanding of the Council of Nicaea is the dispute that surrounds a priest called Arius and his bishop Alexander in the city of Alexandria.[14] Around about the year 318 (but perhaps as late as 322), a conflict arose between Arius and Alexander concerning the very nature of God. Simply put, the argument was centred on the relationship between God the Father and the Son. Alexander held that God was always Father and that the Son was always Son, which implied that the Son was eternally generated, that is, the Son must always have been with the Father. At the same time, Alexander also argued that the Son is the image of the Father and, as such, reveals, represents and shares the same being as the Father. For Arius, this appeared to contradict the biblical insistence that God the Father alone was immortal (e.g. 1 Tim. 6:16), which compromised the unity of God as well as the unique status of the Father. Against Alexander, Arius held that the very language of Father and Son presupposed that the Son was inferior to and derived from the Father, which meant that the Son existed only through the Father's will and not eternally and, furthermore, that the Son did not share the Father's being. In essence, this was a conflict about the status of the Son in which two engaged parties each argued that the other's position distorted and changed the traditional understanding of the faith contained in the scriptural witness and thereby risked altering Christian practice.

What began as a theological controversy between a priest and a bishop built up steam to such an extent that, after a number of smaller intervening councils (two of which vindicated Arius), the new Emperor Constantine took an interest in the dispute, likely through the persuasion of some close advisors. In 325 Constantine convened a council that met from May to July in Nicaea to address the dispute between Arius and Alexander alongside other matters, notably to settle the question of how to devise a method to decide the date of Easter. Because we have no surviving detailed minutes of the Council of Nicaea, as we do of later councils, we are forced to reconstruct the proceedings from scraps of evidence according to which even the number of bishops in attendance is ambiguous, although Eusebius of Caesarea's estimate of about 250 is thought to be generally reliable. What we do have, however, is the ultimate decision of the council against Arius in the form of a short statement of faith:

> We believe in one God, Father Almighty Maker of all things, seen and unseen; and in one Lord Jesus Christ the Son of God, begotten as only begotten of the Father, that is of the being of the Father, God of God, Light of Light, true God of true God, begotten not made, consubstantial with the Father, through whom all things came into existence, both things in heaven and things on earth; who for us men and for our salvation came down and was incarnate and became man, suffered and rose again the third day, ascended in the heavens, and is coming to judge the living and the dead.
>
> And in the Holy Spirit.
>
> But those who say 'there was a time when he did not exist', and 'before being begotten he did not exist', and that he came into being from non-existence, or who allege that the Son of God is from another *hypostasis* or *ousia*, or is alterable or changeable, these the Catholic and Apostolic Church condemns.[15]

In the context of the council, what is most important is the affirmation that the Son is eternally generated from the same *ousia* (substance, essence or being) as the Father and is therefore *homoousios* (of the same substance) with the Father. After the council, Arius along with some of his supporters were exiled; however, within a few years they were recalled and readmitted to communion.

In the wake of Nicaea, what is particularly important for our purposes is to note the sense in which the acceptance of the creed as a normative and authoritative statement of Christian faith was only a very gradual and fragmented process. Recent patristic scholarship has emphasized not only that the drafting of the creed in the first place was *not* done with the intention that it serve as a universal and binding statement of Christian faith but also that even when it became more established in liturgical contexts in the fifth century it did not exclude the local creeds proper to local churches.[16] In other words, the ongoing task of discernment was firmly lodged in local congregations and not promulgated from on high. The evidence we possess also seems to indicate that the council itself never intended the creed to be anything more than an ad hoc statement designed to address a particular conflict within the church.[17] Moreover, what the legacy of Nicaea makes clear is certainly not any easy compromise of the church with imperial power but rather an intensification of the question of the church's own identity and mission that required a creative re-imagination and improvisation of the scriptural witness.[18] It is only through these painful processes of 'making difficult' a gospel message that has been buried under familiarities and platitudes that we are capable of reading Scripture and the tradition with integrity.

Returning to Nicaea, what, then, is the significance of the eternal generation of the Son and of the affirmation that the Son is of the same substance as the Father? And, what are we to make of the scant reference to the Spirit in the Nicene formulation? Exactly what is the problem in the first place and how is the doctrine of the Trinity supposed to help? Underneath the ever-increasing levels of sophistication and technical terminology, the issue can be understood on a hermeneutical level, that is, it can be seen as a way to hold seemingly contradictory biblical narratives together. At its most basic, the problem is about how to reconcile the Christian claim to worship the God of Israel, about whom the most basic confession is 'Hear, O Israel: the LORD our God, the LORD is one' (Deut. 6:4, NKJV), with the divinity of Christ. Put even more crudely, the problem is how to reconcile Jewish monotheism with the claim that Jesus Christ is Lord. According to the biblical narrative, we are forbidden from worshipping any being other than the one true God (e.g. Exod. 20:3–5; Isa. 42:8) so Jesus is only worthy of worship if he is God. However, the biblical text also makes it clear that the Father deserves our worship (e.g. Matt. 7:21; John 2:16) and that Jesus is not the Father (e.g. Matt. 24:36; Luke 22:42; John 1:14). This creates a uniquely Christian problem because it seems that if we want to worship both the Father and the Son then we must admit that the Father is God and that Jesus is God but we cannot say that Jesus is the Father nor can we say that there are two Gods. The same problem obtains with respect to the Spirit (e.g. John 14:26; Rom. 8:26–7). So it appears that we are faced with quite a conundrum because what is required, namely distinction in unity, seems on the surface like a logical impossibility.

One way to see how this was addressed is to briefly look at a later improvisation that further developed the Nicene language of *ousia* and *hypostasis* and, in the course of doing so, made a significant contribution to the development of the doctrine of the Trinity. In one of his many letters, Basil of Caesarea argues that the Trinity is the central mystery at the heart of Christian discipleship by linking it directly to Jesus' injunction to baptize in the name of the Father and of the Son and of the Holy Spirit (Matt. 28:19):

> Since baptism has been given to us by the Savior in the name of the Father and of the Son and of the Holy Spirit, we offer a confession of faith consistent with our baptism, and also the doxology consistent with our faith, glorifying the Holy Spirit with the Father and the Son.[19]

It is generally agreed that Basil along with the other so-called 'Cappadocian Fathers', which include Gregory Nazienzen and Basil's younger brother Gregory of Nyssa, played a pivotal role in establishing the divinity of the Holy Spirit, which was affirmed at the Council of Constantinople in 381, and paved the way for a full statement of the doctrine of the Trinity. While there are still significant differences in their respective positions and in how they articulate them, for our purposes it is nevertheless helpful to draw out their commonalities. Chief among these is the refinement of the Nicene language of *ousia* and *hypostasis*, which the Cappadocians put to good use in illuminating the paradox of unity and diversity in the Godhead. Crudely put, we can say that the Cappadocians argued that the one Godhead exists in three different 'persons'. The divine unity is thus preserved because the three 'persons' (*hypostasis*) are all of the same substance (*ousia*). Crucial to this distinction between substance and person is that whatever is said of the divine nature is true of each of the three persons equally and that the three persons work inseparably. The development of the doctrine of the Trinity is thus an attempt to display the richness and unfathomable depth of the God revealed in Scripture.

Analogies of the Trinity

As is wont to happen in the course of repeatedly trying to explain something that is essentially mysterious and will always remain so, discussions about the doctrine of the Trinity invariably employ a variety of analogies. These are notoriously slippery and must be approached with caution, not least because they can illuminate only some particular aspect of the Trinity, at best, and are often deployed with the express purpose of pointing to inadequacies in other analogies or accompanied by caveats that place strict limits on their explanatory power. To cite but one example, in a letter to his younger brother, Gregory of Nyssa, Basil suggests that we might understand the difference between *ousia* and *hypostasis* by comparing the Trinity to the brilliance of a rainbow, which he suggests is both continuous and divided.[20] Improvising on the description of the Son as the reflection of God's glory (Heb. 1:3) and the Nicene formulation 'light of light', Basil observes that a rainbow allows us to see distinct colours that are, nevertheless, seamlessly part of the same sunbeam and in this way illuminates for us the paradox of distinction in unity characteristic of the Godhead. While this analogy might capture our imaginations and illuminate some aspect of the mystery of the doctrine of the Trinity, it is not long before cracks start to appear and Basil himself explicitly notes that there can never be a complete correspondence between an analogy and what it points toward but only of something vaguely perceptible.

It is perhaps at this point that we would do well to recall Augustine's word of caution that speculation about the doctrine of the Trinity is fraught with danger and the likelihood of error is ever-present. This is nowhere truer than in the case of analogies of the Trinity that have seeped into popular consciousness. Among the most well known of these is the 'water' analogy, according to which just as water takes three forms, namely solid, liquid and vapour, so too God takes the form of Father, Son and Holy Spirit. While at first this may seem helpful for understanding how God is three-in-one, upon further examination it detracts from rather than enhances our understanding of the doctrine of the Trinity. This is because ice, liquid and vapour are three *states* in which a single substance, water, may be found, and to say that God is like this is to radically play down the difference between the three persons by suggesting that the one God is merely made manifest in three different forms. In essence, the 'water' analogy points toward a non-Trinitarian concept of God that leads to what has become known as the heresy of modalism, which is historically associated most closely with the third-century priest Sabellius. If we wanted to make an analogy to do with water we would do better to follow Gregory of Nyssa's suggestion in his book *On the Holy Spirit* that the Trinity is analogous to a spring as a source of water: 'starting from that Source as from a spring pouring life abundantly, through the Only-begotten Who is the True life, by the operation of the Holy Spirit'.[21] Though we may distinguish between the fount, spring and stream the one flows from the other and all are of the same substance, namely water.

Further reflecting on the difficulty of the mystery of the Trinity, Augustine observes that 'because the Father is not the Son and the Son is not the Father, and the Holy Spirit who is also called *the gift of God* (Acts 8:20; John 4:10) is neither the Father nor the Son, they are certainly three. Yet when you ask "Three what?" human speech labors under a great dearth of words. So we say three persons, not in order to say that precisely, but in order not to be reduced to silence.'[22] Beginning, then, from the weight of scriptural authority that affirms God is love (e.g. 1 John 4:8–16), Augustine suggests that we may conceive of the Trinity as the relation between the mind, its knowledge and its love of self.

> And so you have a certain image of the trinity, the mind itself and its knowledge, which is its offspring and its word about itself, and love as the third element, and these *three are one* (1 John 5:8) and are one substance. Nor is the offspring less than the mind so long as the mind knows itself as much as it is, nor is love any less so along as it loves itself as much as it knows and as much as it is.[23]

For Augustine, the mind cannot love itself unless it also knows itself and so these three are all fundamentally united as one. Reflecting on the mutuality and equality between the three persons, Augustine makes the crucial link to a life of discipleship by suggesting that just as they 'keep the unity of the Spirit in the bond of peace (Eph. 4:3) . . . we are bidden to imitate this mutuality by grace, both with reference to God and to each other, in the two precepts on which the whole law and the prophets depend (Matt. 22:40)'.[24] If, then, as the apostle wrote, the love of God has been poured into our hearts through the Holy Spirit who has been given to us (Rom. 5:5) then the Christian life itself is inexorably drawn toward participation in this complex divine economy of the giving and receiving of love between ourselves and God, our neighbours and our enemies (Matt. 5:43–4).

Practising Trinitarian Theology

We began this chapter by suggesting that an understanding of the doctrine of the Trinity has the potential to rejuvenate a life of Christian discipleship today and while our brief sketch will have hopefully illuminated at least to some small extent why it was generative for early Christianity its continuing importance may be less clear. Indeed, one of the giants of modern philosophy, Immanuel Kant, argues that 'the doctrine of the Trinity, taken literally, has no practical relevance at all, even if we think we understand it; and it is even more clearly irrelevant if we realize that it transcends all our concepts. Whether we are to worship three or ten persons in the Deity makes no difference.'[25] Modern theologians, too, have cast serious doubt on whether the Trinity is of any use in the elaboration of Christian doctrine and many wonder, as Frederich Schleiermacher did, if deductions about the Trinity should not simply be put aside as 'philosophemes' that are plagued with inconsistencies.²⁶

Often flying directly in the face of these two influential giants, there has more recently been a raft of theologians enlisting support for particular kinds of communities precisely through and on the basis of arguments about how we are to understand the doctrine of the Trinity. Particularly within the last three decades or so, the Trinity has become something of a *locus classicus* around which a vision for social life is developed by unpacking the unity and diversity of the Trinitarian relations in a variety of different ways. As in the case of using analogies to understand the doctrine of the Trinity, however, it is often the case that whatever socio-political potential is harnessed by analyses of Trinitarian operations is one-sided at best and self-deceptive at worst.²⁷ Here again we would do well to heed the same kind of caution that Augustine recommends and not jump too hastily to a simplistic kind of imitation of our own flawed interpretation of what is, in the end, a truth glimpsed only darkly through a veil.

With that in mind, then, we would like to conclude this chapter with the suggestion that peacemaking can be enlivened and strengthened if we understand it as a Trinitarian practice. If we understand the Triune God as a God not of disorder but of peace (1 Cor. 14:33) then our participation in the divine economy must also be characterized by peace. In his wonderful book, *These Three are One*, David Cunningham points toward just the kind of embodiment of Trinitarian practice that we have in mind:

> In its affirmation of difference that does not devolve into strife, the doctrine of the Trinity establishes the theological priority of peace. God is internally differentiated, but the resulting potentiality for conflict is faced and negotiated by means of mutual love and abundant donation – not through coercion, strife or violence. In this polyphonic orchestration of oneness and difference, Christian thought finds its highest good and greatest perfection.²⁸

It is important to note here that this vision is essentially an eschatological one, that is, although the Christian tradition points us toward the Triune God in whom peace is always already realized, here below we can, at best, reflect and long for such a peaceable kingdom and lament when its final restoration does not seem forthcoming any time soon. Granted, there is no prescription here for a plan of action but this is as it should be because, contrary to some, the Trinity is not a model for human living in the sense that it is offered simply for us to imitate based on our extrapolations of how divine relations are applicable to us. Rather, if we are to practise Trinitarian theology with integrity, we must train ourselves to participate in the life of the Triune God, which is most explicitly revealed to us in the life and work of Jesus Christ, the Lamb who was slaughtered. It should go without saying that the difficult work of making peace, of living out Isaiah's vision of the day that the lion will lie down with the lamb (Isa. 11:6–9), cannot be confined to some special interest group or a particular denomination. The art of peacemaking is an ecclesial task because its provenance is to be found in the nature of the Triune God. This insight has recently been vividly affirmed in a document drafted by the Vatican's International Theological Commission that seeks to 'illustrate, on the basis of the truth of Jesus Christ, the relationship between the revelation of God and a non-violent humanism ... by reconsidering the Trinitarian confession of the one God and the implications of the revelation of Christ for the redemption of the bond between human beings'.[29] That an understanding of non-violence and reconciliation is being pursued as arising from the very nature of the Triune God is surely a cause for celebration and hope.

5.

Speaking of God

> If you have grasped what you want to say, it is not God. If you have been able to comprehend it, you have comprehended something other than God. If you think you have been able to comprehend it in a way, your thought deceives you. If you have comprehended it, that is not it; if that is it, you have not comprehended it. What, therefore, is it that you want to say about what you are not able to comprehend?
>
> – Saint Augustine (354–430)[1]

Speaking of the Incomprehensible God

All speech about God is difficult, not because God presents a particularly difficult intellectual problem but rather because we are trying to speak about what we cannot comprehend. That the discipline of talking about God – literally theology – has such a long, complex and ongoing history is at least somewhat remarkable if the object of its speech is incomprehensible. Why do we go on attempting to speak of that which cannot be comprehended? Augustine suggests that 'although nothing can be spoken in a way worthy of God, he has sanctioned the homage of the human voice, and chosen that we should derive pleasure from our words in praise of him'.[2] Worship itself is the basic context in which our speech of God is given voice in prayer, song and praise.

All attempts to speak of the incomprehensible God thus stand on something of a precipice: on the one hand, since all our speech is necessarily inadequate there is the temptation to simply resort to silence and, on the other hand, since God welcomes our speaking there is the temptation to say too much. Each of these two temptations are equally problematic because in the first case, God can become the ineffable sublime about whom nothing whatsoever can be reasonably said and, in the second case, God can be transformed into a mythical supreme being that looks an awful lot like us. Likewise, the consequences of these two temptations are equally disastrous. In the first case God is so completely Other that what we are left with is some version of deism where God simply leaves us to our own devices and is therefore largely irrelevant or, in the second case, if God is to be 'useful' or engaged in the world then we must conceive of God as possessing human characteristics, albeit in the highest degree. In both cases, however, the god thus described would no longer be God but an idol of our making. The burden of this chapter will be to show that the Christian tradition of speaking of God avoids both these temptations by understanding its speech within the context of a fundamental distinction between Creator and creatures. The consequences of failing to adequately adjust our speech in the light of this distinction are serious indeed, as we will see later in the book.

Attending to the Written Word

If we are to speak well of God, or at least as well as finite creatures are able, we can do no better than to begin, as early Christianity as well as the Fathers and the scholastics did, from the scriptural witness. What we see throughout the biblical narrative is the inseparability of life and language or, perhaps better, that the very act of speaking is life itself coming to expression. This connection is made abundantly clear, for example, in the covenant with Abraham in which the speech on Sinai serves as the means to declare the life-giving bond between God and the people (Exod. 19 – 20). The essential link between life and language continues in the words of the prophets, which became the concrete vehicle through which God's engagement with the people was communicated, and finds its culmination in the event of the Word of God becoming flesh in Jesus Christ (John 1:14). Indeed, if humanity is made in the image of God (Gen. 1:26–7) and the Son is the image of the Father (Col. 1:15) then we can legitimately conclude that all of our speaking is a particular expression of an impression of the form of Christ. One of the most vivid aspects of the incarnation, however, is that when the Word became flesh it was not simply to speak to us but rather to live among us, to dwell with us or, to borrow a potent Hebrew metaphor, to set up a tent with us (Exod. 25:8; echoed in John 1:14), albeit in a much more intimate way than in the desert.

The question that presses itself upon us in the light of this overwhelming gift of God is how and in what ways our limited human words can faithfully express the limitless divine truth the incarnate Logos is sent to make known. The difficulty here cannot be underestimated since it appears that Jesus himself longs to reveal much more than his often hopelessly wooden disciples can understand (John 16:12). Moreover, this difficulty of speaking of the ways of God is also illuminated in Jesus' foretelling of his own death (Matt. 20:17–19; Mark 10:32–4; Luke 18:31–4), which cannot be captured in words and becomes rather the silent event that gives rise to a dearth of speaking that knows no possible end. Helpfully making the Trinitarian connection, Hans Urs von Balthasar suggests that:

> in all this, the seemingly finite content of what he [Jesus] says (in whatever form he may speak), and thus the realms of silence that remain in it, are handed over to an ongoing, never to be ended hermeneutic of the Holy Spirit within the history of the Church. The Spirit is capable of taking what seems unspoken within the spoken and of fitting it into always new words that deepen and explain, without, for all that, ever coming to an end.[3]

Our speaking about the incomprehensible God, who is made known to us most vividly though the person and work of Jesus Christ, the incarnate Word made flesh, is made possible by the creative and improvisational work of the Spirit who enables our finite words to participate, however imperfectly, in the infinite life of the Triune God.

The Fundamental Distinction

At first, it might seem strange to suggest, as we want to in this chapter, that the Christian life itself is lived in the light of a distinction that is narrated in the most concrete way for us in the gospels.⁴ Such an emphasis on a distinction, indeed on one particular distinction between God and the world, may be of some special interest to theologians and philosophers but that contemplation of it could be more than a theoretical pursuit seems, at least on the surface, a piece of academic wishful thinking. However, to marginalize the practical importance of distinctions is to overlook the sense in which human life is led by distinguishing one thing from another. Examples abound here and range from the essential distinctions that enable us to classify and differentiate parts of the created world, such as distinctions of quality, quantity, relation and so on, to moral distinctions between good, evil, right and wrong. Moreover, our ability to make such distinctions depends on them first being there for us to discover, that is to say, distinctions first arise in the course of living. For our purposes, we may infer from this that the Christian life is led in the light of the distinction between God and the world that was given to us and expressed most vividly in the person and work of Jesus Christ.

This fundamental Christian distinction between God and the world has occupied the reflections of a great number of theologians and philosophers down the centuries and has been expressed in a host of different ways and contexts. One clear expression of this distinction is found in Book VII of Augustine's *Confessions* where he narrates what was for him one of the most profound shifts in his understanding of God. For us, Augustine's account of this shift is particularly helpful not only because it is written in what is a more familiar narrative style but also because he helpfully distinguishes his understanding of God from the pagan understanding so prevalent in his day. Augustine tells us that he had originally felt forced to conceive of God as something physically extended, something that permeated infinite space but that was nevertheless incorruptible, inviolable and unchangeable. The problem that Augustine sees with this conception of God, however, is that if God is some kind of infinite material object then this implies that God is divisible, which contradicts his earlier conviction that God is 'wonderfully simple'.⁵ For Augustine, to say that God is 'wonderfully simple' means that we cannot imagine that God is in the possession of beauty or greatness; God simply *is* beauty and greatness. There is no division in God between his being and his attributes. Through reading some 'books of the Platonists' Augustine tells us that he came to a new conception of God that avoided his earlier errors.

> By the Platonic books I was admonished to return into myself. With you as my guide I entered into my innermost citadel, and was given the power to do so because you had become my helper (Ps. 29:11). I entered and with my soul's eye, such as it was, saw above that same eye of my soul the immutable light higher than my mind – not the light of every day, obvious to anyone, nor a larger version of the same kind which would, as it were, have given out a much brighter light and filled everything with its magnitude. It was not that light, but a different thing, utterly different from all our kinds of light. It transcended my mind, not in the way that oil floats on water, nor as heaven is above earth. It was superior because it made me, and I was inferior because I was made by it. When I first came to know you, you raised me up to make me see that what I saw was Being, and that I who saw am not yet Being. And you gave a shock to the weakness of my sight by the strong radiance of your rays, and I trembled with love and awe. And I found myself far from you 'in the region of dissimilarity', and heard as it were your voice from on high: 'I am the food of the fully grown; grow and you will feed on me. And you will not change me into you like the food your flesh eats, but you will be changed into me.'[6]

As this passage makes clear, Augustine no longer conceives of God as something that can be compared on any level with the things of the world. Put simply, Augustine comes to the realization that God is not a Being among beings. This basic fact is what makes all our speaking of God very difficult indeed.

The significance of this insight, that God is 'utterly different', cannot be underestimated. The pagan view of the world from which Augustine distinguishes his own conception of God held that distinctions are made within the context of the world in which one thing is capable of being differentiated from another. The creator god is conceived of as a 'demiurge' or 'craftsman' that brings order within this single whole, which is not further distinguished from anything beyond it.[7] This demiurge is indeed an intelligent designer, a cosmic craftsman, but is nothing more than a causal force that shapes the world in space and time. The distinction that Augustine wants to make takes the whole of the pagan view of the world and uses it as one of the terms of the distinction between creator and creatures. While the demiurge may indeed be a benevolent craftsman, this god is no creator in the theological sense but merely one who can impose order. The distinction that Augustine is at pains to emphasize is the one between Being and beings or, if you like, between the Creator and that which is made. For Augustine, all things that are not Being exist only by participation in a radically transcendent God who is the ground and possibility of all creaturely existence in the first place. The God Augustine is describing is the infinite and eternal creative act of Being that sustains all things in their finite existence.

What this fundamentally Christian distinction requires is nothing less than a radical readjustment of the language we use when we talk about God. Whereas according to the pagan view everything, including the cosmic craftsman, is capable of identification precisely because it can be distinguished from something else the Christian distinction understands God to be entirely beyond any such relation to the world. This is helpfully illuminated by Maximus the Confessor (580–662) who suggests that whereas the being of finite things has non-being as its opposite, God's being is beyond any such opposition.[8] This is why Augustine says that God's transcendence is unlike the way oil floats on water, because God is beyond any distinction whatsoever. What this implies is that, in the Christian understanding, God is not established as God by a distinction whereas pagan gods are established by being distinguished from other things. This basic principle, that God is not a Being among beings, means that speaking of God will never be a straightforward matter because the vast majority of our speaking is about things that are part of this world and God is not part of the world but the creator of the world. However, we are convinced that because the Word of God lived among us (John 1:14) and has spoken to us by a Son (Heb. 1:2) that, like Peter and John, we cannot keep from speaking about what we have seen and heard (Acts 4:20).

A Way Out of Silence

If we are to go on speaking of God it seems that we are left in quite a predicament. How can we possibly go on to speak of the God who is not a Being among beings? This vexing dilemma is eloquently described by the psalmist, who writes that in the proclamation of all creation 'there is no speech, nor are there words; their voice is not heard; yet their voice goes out though all the earth, and their words to the end of the world' (Ps. 19:3–4). How is it possible to speak with an inaudible voice? How is it possible, that is to say, for our finite words to conform to the infinite gift of God given to us in Jesus Christ? At this point, we can turn for help to one of the greatest thinkers the Christian tradition has so far produced, namely Saint Thomas Aquinas (c. 1225–74). If we attend, more specifically, to his understanding of how theological language works we will be able to see how it is possible to steer a path between falling silent and saying too much.

Throughout his work, Aquinas is concerned to develop an account of how we are able to speak of the incomprehensible God. Like Augustine, he acknowledges that our speech about God will always be inadequate but maintains that it can nevertheless be true speech. Aquinas claims this is possible by making some further distinctions about how we use language in the context of our speaking about God who is not a Being among beings. The critical juncture is found in his *Summa Theologiae* when he asks how and in what ways it is possible to name God.[9] In the course of his exploration, Aquinas distinguishes between three different uses of language, which enables us to speak meaningfully and truthfully of the God who is beyond naming, allowing us to affirm that words like 'good' and 'wise' truly characterize God while, at the same time, acknowledging that these words fail to represent God adequately. In the face of numerous problems and objections, Aquinas suggests that:

> words are used analogically of God and creatures, not purely equivocally and not purely univocally; for our only words for God come from creatures, as we have said, and so whatever we say of God and creatures is said in virtue of the relationship creatures bear to God as to the source and cause in which all their creaturely perfections pre-exist in a more excellent way.[10]

The difference between using words analogically, equivocally and univocally is the crucial one to understand and while it may seem complicated at first it is actually quite straightforward and allows us to navigate the difficult path between silence and saying too much in our speech about God.

We use words univocally when a word means exactly the same thing in more than one case. So, for example, if we say 'Thomas is a man, and Brian and Kyle are also' we are predicating exactly the same thing of Thomas, Brian and Kyle, namely that they are all men. We use words equivocally when the same word takes on a totally different meaning. Take the following two sentences, for example: 'I love apricot jam' and 'There was a terrible jam on the motorway this evening'. In these two sentences the same word, 'jam', has two completely different meanings because it would be nonsense to think that there could be an apricot-flavoured traffic back-up or to complain about the consequences of finding a particular fruit preserve on a road.

The issue Aquinas draws our attention to is that because all our speech about God is couched in creaturely terms and God is not a creature we cannot speak of God either univocally or equivocally. If we understand our theological language as univocal then 'God is good' and 'chocolate is good' would both use the word 'good' in exactly the same way, which would have the effect of mistaking God for just another thing in the world. Thus if we understand our speech about God univocally we would be attempting the impossible because, as we have seen, God cannot be fully comprehended or described in this way. Any attempt of this sort, of which there are more and more in our day of fashionable atheisms, would, therefore, fall short of being speech about God at all because all it would describe is a cosmic craftsman, a mere supreme being. On the other hand, if we understand our theological language as equivocal then 'God is love' and 'Christians must love' would use the word 'love' in completely different ways. Thus if we understand our speech about God equivocally we would, in effect, be rendered speechless. Any attempt of this sort makes the deist mistake and assumes that God is absent from the world and has no relation to creation. All our speaking of the God who is not a Being among beings must therefore be on constant alert to these two problematic uses of theological language lest it be tempted to say too much (univocal language) or fall silent (equivocal language).

For Aquinas, then, theological language is neither univocal nor equivocal. When we speak truly of God, which we do in fact, we are neither capturing God in language nor failing to say anything about God whatsoever. Instead of either of these, Aquinas suggests that all our language about God is analogical because it has a different meaning but one that is nevertheless related in some way. Speaking of God analogically means ' that we can use words to mean more than they mean to us – that we can use words to "try to mean" what God is like, that we can reach out to God with our words even though they do not circumscribe what He is'.[11] Situated between univocity and equivocity, between saying too much and falling silent, Aquinas's concept of analogy seems to preserve some of our intuitions about the ongoing relationship between God and the world, the most powerful of which are attested to in Scripture. If we say that 'God is good' and 'Mother Teresa is good', for example, it is clear that although we cannot use the word 'good' in exactly the same way with respect to God and creatures there does seem to be some relationship because we want to say that Mother Teresa's goodness is somehow related to God's.

Perhaps the single most important key to understanding Aquinas's idea of analogical language is that all of creation stands in a real relation to God and thus in some way bears the imprint of its creator. Because creatures are caused by God they are, so to speak, God's effects and thus cannot help but resemble God in some way. For Aquinas, all things in the world reflect or reveal something of God because God is their cause. On this basis, we can indeed speak truthfully of God but, Aquinas cautions, whatever we say about God will always be exemplified differently in creatures. We may say, for example, that 'God is good' and 'Mother Teresa is good' but we must also insist that Mother Teresa *has* goodness while God *is* the source and origin of goodness itself. That is, whatever measure of goodness is exemplified by Mother Teresa comes from God as the source and origin of goodness and while we can say with a measure of precision what it is that makes Mother Teresa good, when we use the word 'good' to describe God we are speaking truthfully yet our words in this case exceed our ability to know what they mean. In this sense we both do and do not understand what we are saying when we talk about God.

Reflecting on Aquinas's use of analogy, Herbert McCabe helpfully points out that in theological language words are:

> things that are destroyed in use. The theologian uses a word by stretching it to breaking point, and it is precisely as it breaks that the communication, if any, is achieved. He takes a perfectly good pagan word like 'God' or 'sacred' or 'prayer' and twists it out of all recognition: and he does this not from verbal sadism but because there are not any other words to use.[12]

This is why all theological language is, at best, analogical because we can speak only in fractured, imperfect ways that infer God's perfections from those reflected in what God has made. This is also why our talk of God will never be as straightforward and uncomplicated as we might like. Indeed, as Aquinas says:

> God is both simple, like a form, and subsistent, like a concrete thing, and so we sometimes refer to him by abstract nouns to indicate his simplicity and sometimes by concrete nouns to indicate his subsistence and completeness; though neither way of speaking measures up to his way of being, for in this life we do not know him as he is in himself.[13]

All our speaking of the incomprehensible God, then, will necessarily have to be extremely flexible and will indeed, as McCabe suggests, stretch our creaturely language to the limit. That we can speak truthfully of God and are not reduced to the silence of equivocity is, however, surely a means of grace made possible by the overwhelming gift of God, the creator, speaking to us in the person and work of Jesus Christ.

The Lost Art of Being a Creature

If, as we have been arguing, the life of Christian discipleship must be lived in the light of a radical distinction between God and the world it remains to be seen what difference this fundamental distinction makes. What we want to suggest is that our understanding of this distinction between God and the world has profound and far-reaching effects for how we conceive of issues central to human life itself: What is the creaturely context in which we live? What constitutes human sociality from this perspective and how does it relate to other non-human parts of the created order? How do we understand our relationship to animals and other ecological spheres of life? How are the goods of the created order to be shared? If creation is radically dependent on its creator are there natural laws that can be discovered in the ordering of creation itself? New developments in cosmology and physics – popularized recently in the confirmation of the Higgs boson, the ineptly named 'God particle' – coupled with the increasing realization of the gravity of our environmental crisis have brought reflection on creation to the forefront of our collective thinking in recent decades. However, this reflection is often confused, perhaps especially so in theological quarters because it does not wrestle seriously enough with the distinction between God and the world.

One way of getting to the heart of what is at stake here might be to enumerate the ways in which this fundamental distinction can be received as good news. If we look to the recent history of Christianity, however, the answer is quite clear that this distinction is highly suspect. Indeed, it takes only a little digging to unearth the thoroughly repugnant fact that much of the violence, hatred and exclusion manifested in our world is covertly underwritten by a perverse doctrine of creation. The political terrors unleashed by twisting and forming the fundamental distinction between God and the world into something that justifies violence and exclusion is for our purposes helpfully seen in the rise of National Socialism in Germany. We have already referred to this in Chapter 2, but here we can be more specific because the political order under Hitler was legitimated in part through an appeal to creation, which is both validated by God and applicable universally. Indeed, the *Deutsche Christen* movement within German Protestantism sought to align itself with the ideological principles of Nazism on the basis of an appeal to the orders of creation by arguing that 'God's order could be discovered in the natural conditions of nation and race, and that his will could be seen in the event of Hitler's seizure of power'.[14] Christian support was thereby offered for a racist order that excluded 'the other' (the Jew, the homosexual, the mentally disabled, etc.) and divided humanity into separate identifiable peoples on the basis that this ordering was part of God's blessing in creation. In this specific context it was Dietrich Bonhoeffer who realized that from this perspective 'one need only to hold out something as God-created for it to be vindicated for ever, the division of man into nations, national struggles, war, class struggle, the exploitation of the weak by the strong, the cut-throat competition of economics.'[15] Though this is, perhaps, the example that has captured our collective imaginations most there are many others we could mention, such as the case of apartheid in South Africa or the genocide in Rwanda.

More problematic still is that these problems are not restricted to horrific events that seem to us in hindsight and at a safe enough remove to be clearly at odds with the gospel. The appeal to creation is often invoked to justify unjust socio-political arrangements, which are subsequently ascribed to God. Stanley Hauerwas is rightly suspicious of the extent to which these kinds of arguments make it more difficult for us to accept the existence of those who do not agree with us and thereby end up making the resort to violence and coercion more understandable. The appeal to universal rights, for example, seems to embody the highest human ideal but, precisely because of this, also makes possible the argument that a denial of these rights is inhuman and that anyone holding such inhuman views must be forced to change their mind. Hauerwas rightly points out that appeals to creation often 'function as an ideology for sustaining some Christians' presuppositions that their societies – particularly societies of Western democracies – are intrinsic to God's purposes'.[16] The 'logic' of this position is also what, in the end, justified the invasion of Iraq in the face of massive protests in Washington and London.

If it is the case that the doctrine of creation is so susceptible to misuse and distortion, what is to be done? What we want to suggest is that the legitimation of unjust social orders and the justification of violence that arise in certain appeals to creation result from a failure to wrestle seriously with the profound implications of the distinction between creator and creation. By making this point we are not trying to absolve or sidestep the long tradition of oppression and violence – of both humanity and nature – that is powerfully present and legitimated in Christendom. Our sympathies lie rather with Grace Jantzen who suggests that our task must be to 'discern *both* how Christendom from its foundational texts has legitimated and valorized violence *and* how it provides resources for creativity and peace'.[17] Our conviction is that while we have been quite attentive to the former we have for too long neglected the latter and that this imbalance is in urgent need of attention if we are to participate in God's project of reconciliation.

What we want to suggest, then, is that careful attention to the way we speak about God can and does place all of our speech in the context of a fundamental distinction between creator and creation, which means that we must learn to speak *as creatures*. By understanding ourselves *as creatures* we become able to place ourselves within God's story in which all of creation is being reconciled to God through Jesus Christ (Col. 1:20).

Here again, as has been the case throughout, we can only gesture toward some of the important considerations. Chief among these is that God does not create out of any need. That is to say, all of creation is contingent, radically dependent on God and not in any way necessary. Creation is the free and unconstrained act of God and all of creation is entirely the result of God's loving action.[18] Understood as a relation of radical dependence, then, creation simply names all of reality as existing only in relation to a creator. In the Christian tradition this has been described as creation *ex nihilo*, or creation out of nothing. Rowan Williams makes the further suggestion that 'God's relation to the whole world is like this: not a struggle with pre-existing disorder that is then moulded into shape, but a pure summons. "My hand laid the foundation of the earth, and my right hand spread out the heavens; when I call to them, they stand forth together" (Is. 48:13).'[19] This has some vital implications. Perhaps most importantly, it means quite emphatically that creation is not any kind of imposition or manipulation. God does not create by imposing order because prior to God's word there literally is nothing to impose order on. This also gives the lie to uncritical notions of God's 'monarchy' because, as the free loving act of God, creation has no need to be governed in this way. To put it another way, our radical dependence on God is not the dependence of enslavement but rather a dependence that enables us to be creatures. 'Being creatures is learning humility, not as submission to an alien will, but as the acceptance of limit and death; *for* that acceptance, with all that it means in terms of our moral imagination and action, we are equipped by learning through the grace of Christ and the concrete fellowship of the Spirit, that God is "the desire by which all live", the *creator*.'[20] Perhaps the most adequate words that can be spoken of God, then, take the form of thanksgiving: 'I give you thanks, O LORD, with my whole heart; before the gods I sing your praise; I bow down toward your holy temple and give thanks to your name for your steadfast love and your faithfulness; for you have exalted your name and your word above everything (Ps. 138:1–2).

6.

God, Faith and Knowledge

Thanks be you, Lord, Jesus Christ,
for all the benefits which you have won for us,
for all the pains and insults you have born for us.
O most merciful Redeemer, Friend and Brother,
may we know you more clearly,
love you more dearly,
and follow you more nearly, day by day.
– Richard of Chichester (1197–1253)

On Knowing What You're Talking About

In this chapter we come to questions about faith and knowledge of God. It is possible that some readers might think this should have come much earlier. After all this talk about God, how do we know what we are talking about? This is a question that should have been settled at the start. Christian believers and all kinds of theologians speak of knowledge of God but what does this mean, and how do they know? Surely it would have been better to set out the foundations on which we then built our talk about God?

We are aware that a widely held contemporary belief implies that if you know something you can demonstrate the truth of it. You can prove it. It is on this basis that the great fruitful enterprise of modern science has given such good and rich results. Christian believers, however, cannot take this route with God. That has been our argument because God is not something, a member of a class of objects, some part of the world we can examine and demonstrate. We noted that the Bible does not even attempt any argument for God's existence. God is just 'there', the source of all that is, transcending all that is created yet fundamental to all that lives. God is beyond our reach and in the previous chapter on speaking of God we readily recognized our limitation in this regard. It's not that we admit this is a problem about God but rather it is the truth that we embrace. If we could identify God, if we could capture God in our words, then who or whatever we spoke about as God would not be God.

This does not mean that God is unknowable, unspeakable. Although God is beyond our knowing and our words we are not reduced to silence because God has spoken to us. The Elusive One has drawn near and so we have something to say, albeit modestly and with grateful wonder. It may be true that in some cases Christian believers have spoken too stridently, have laid claim in their arguments to truths that they could not know. There are ways of speaking of God that are too confident to be true precisely because they have no sense of the enormity of what they do in speaking of the mystery of God at all. In the name of God they have then gone on to impose themselves and their views on others, sometimes with a violence and hatred which denies the God they claim to know.

For example, there is something disturbing in the story of the conversion of Constantine. In a dream he sees a vision of the cross and marks this sign on the shield of his soldiers. Under this sign he went forth to conquer. He was brought up in a military context so conquering meant war and the killing of enemies. Yet is there not a great oddness, to say the least, in fighting and killing enemies under the sign of Jesus' work of salvation?[1] Later generations of kings and knights were to go on crusades with many deaths resulting, all in the name of Christ. They were confident that this would honour God and that they would have the victory. They prayed for God's blessing and sought God's protection. Was God honoured by this mayhem? We may grant that the knights were sincere but it is possible to be sincerely wrong. It is a sad feature of the history of the church, even to the present day, that Christians have killed pagans and have tortured, imprisoned, burned, hanged and murdered other Christians, all in the name of Christ.

Christians believe God has spoken to us, in the story of Israel and most wonderfully in Jesus. We have the crucial record of this in the Bible. But even in the Bible we find a questioning by one generation of another. Did they really understand the word of the Lord? Was their behaviour really a faithful expression of their calling before God?

Let's look at contrasting views of the same event by a historian and a prophet. The town of Jezreel became a kind of winter capital in the days of King Ahab and Queen Jezebel. It is near the place of confrontation between Ahab and Naboth over the owning of a vineyard, a serious story which results in Elijah confronting the king and the queen and announcing coming judgement. The fulfilment of this word comes as Jehu, specifically anointed to the role by the prophet, comes with wrath, massacring those who supported Ahab and Jezebel (2 Kgs 9 – 10). The story appears in the history as the outworking of God's judgement. It is truly a blood-bath. As such, it embarrasses us. Is speaking this way of God a problem? We need not doubt that it happened but were those involved reading the will of God aright? But we are not the first to be troubled in this way. Some decades later, Hosea the prophet is told by God to name his first son Jezreel (Hos. 1:4), a name symbolizing coming judgement on the house of Jehu. Jehu might well have overthrown the idolatrous house of Ahab but now Jehu's house will fall in disgrace, the ending of the house of Israel. Jezreel is not a name of triumph but of shame. The memory brought sorrow and the warning that we can all get things wrong before God.

Listening to and Interpreting Scripture

Nevertheless, it is to the Bible we turn, rereading its story, hearing the testimony, struggling with the meaning of the call of God. The books of Scripture were written to be read. In that sense we are listening to the witnesses, telling and interpreting the story. It is significant that Israel's basic affirmation of beliefs begins:

> Hear, O Israel: The LORD is our God, the LORD alone. You shall love the LORD your God with all your heart, and with all your soul, and with all your might. Keep these words that I am commanding you today in your heart. Recite them to your children and talk about them

when you are at home and when you are away, when you lie down and when you rise. Bind them as a sign on your hand, fix them as an emblem on your forehead, and write them on the doorposts of your house and on your gates. (Deut. 6:4–9)[2]

God is announced as the source if life. The people are reminded of their essential partnership with God. And the exodus event of liberation is recalled.

It is by hearing, telling and retelling this story that Israel and the children learn about God. We have already noted how a failure to do this leads to disaster in Israel.[3] The story must be told for generations yet unborn (Ps. 78:4). There is an important responsibility laid upon the people of God to teach themselves and their children about God's ways. In this important sense knowledge of God should and can be taught. There is danger in forgetfulness of this story of God (Deut. 4:1–10). In contrast there is the possibility of renewal of Christian life and work through careful listening to Scripture.[4] Of course, we are not really listening at all if we have already decided what God is saying. But if the story of the church is marred by the refusal to listen and the resulting bloodshed it also includes times when often small groups, eagerly attentive to God, have found renewal and faithful courage to walk in new ways of discipleship. We mentioned this possibility in Chapter 3 when we cited the Pilgrim Fathers and their hearing the call of God through fresh reading of Scripture. Through faithful listening, renewal has come. Listening to the witnesses is a crucial part of Christian existence.

As we have said, such renewal is not always welcomed, especially by those guarding a particular aspect of the tradition. And by the same token we must say that not all claimed renewal movements have the Spirit of God about them. So we name a continuing issue for the church. It is about discernment of the ways and will of God. It is easy to shout slogans, like *sola scriptura*, the Bible alone, but we are painfully aware at times that the Bible is heard differently and interpreted differently. Who shall decide? An easy answer is to say, 'The church'. But which 'church', Catholic, Orthodox, Reformed, Pentecostal, Anabaptist? Some of these have departments that decide these issues, for example, the *Magisterium* declares what Catholic Christians are taught to believe. Others traditionally have given serious weight to recognized theologians, especially those of the past, for the example, the Reformed traditions and John Calvin, or Methodism and John Wesley.

All these churches, in varying degrees, attach importance to the tradition of the faith, especially as in the form of the ecumenical creeds of Nicaea, Constantinople and Chalcedon. Some churches include the Apostles' Creed in their celebration of Holy Communion or the Eucharist. That reference to worship is important because it is always a mistake to take any creed as a separate statement of propositions about God, as if such could stand alone and apart from the life of the living church of disciples. The creeds are never final statements of the faith. They require testing against Scripture and stand as important statements of what Christians at one time recognized as the faith they held. Geoffrey Wainwright tells of an occasion in a World Council of Churches study group when a Jamaican Baptist minister, whose denominational stance might have made him wary of such ancient documents, readily declared he recognized his own faith in the words of the creed.[5] The creeds remind us of how Scripture has been used in shaping our understanding of the Christian life. But the time-honoured important distinction must be born in mind: tradition is the living faith of the dead whereas traditionalism is the dead faith of the living. Because we have always done it that way, or believed that way, does not mean that what we are taught is right or wrong. We still have our task of discernment and God may yet have more for us. He does have more for us, so the church is a listening community, to Scripture, to one another in the past and the present, trusting in the Holy Spirit to lead us into the truth. Jesus is the truth (John 14:6). We have already affirmed our conviction that God was in Christ reconciling the world to himself. Jesus is the crucial teacher in the matter of discernment. The Holy Spirit we believe is given to us, to take of the things of Christ and show them to us. That sometimes leads to new insights, challenges to ancient traditions and beliefs.

New Insights

To take one example, Zurich in 1525 was a city of exuberant unrest. Ulrich Zwingli was pastor was of the central church and began to teach and explore the faith under the principle of *sola scriptura*. He led a group of bright students, eager to read the New Testament in Greek together. They also thought about bringing the church more into line with the teaching and practices of the New Testament. They recognized that some of the present teaching of the church was very different from the New Testament, some aspects even being contradictory such as the selling of indulgences. The city council decided for reformation. They decided what was to be preached and practised as the faith of Christians in that place.

The small groups to study the Bible that Zwingli encouraged flourished. There was serious Bible-reading going on and the groups discussed what they read. Church traditions increasingly came under more criticism. The small group meeting with Zwingli became even more penetrating in its thought. Among the members were: Conrad Grebel, son of a leading Zurich family; George Blaurock, a former Catholic priest; Felix Mantz, a gifted linguist skilled in the biblical languages; and Simon Stumpf. This group pressed Zwingli to make reformation changes. The city council became more cautious. Baptism, oath-taking and bearing arms became big issues. Some parents refused to have their babies baptized. The council recalled an old law that made rebaptism nothing less than a capital offence. The pressure increased as the authority of tradition and the council was underlined by force and threat. But on 21 January 1525, in a private home, George Blaurock asked Conrad Grebel to baptize him. Blaurock then baptized the others, on their confession of faith for the remission of sins. It was what they believed was baptism according to the New Testament. It was the beginning of Anabaptism and another way of being church and a different reading of the Scriptures.[6]

Within this single story we see elements that recur again and again in the story of the church before God: the reading of the Bible, the focus on Jesus Christ the Lord, the call to discipleship, faithful following of Jesus, the inspiration of the Holy Spirit, the corporate group nature of faith along with a grace-enabled unforced decision, the costliness of loyalty to Christ and his church. This last point is reflected in the fact that many of those early Anabaptists were martyred. And so we recall that in the name of their gods pagans have killed Christians. And in the name of Christ, Christians have killed Christians. It is that murderous arrogance that we wish to undermine in our call to trust again the living Christ-like God. None of us comes without some blood on our hands. The call to repentance is no light matter.

Trusting the Witnesses

Knowing God involves trusting the witnesses, those in the Bible who told the story of Jesus, his life, death and resurrection, and also those others who followed and lived and died in that trust of God. Sometimes, we think, they were more perceptive and receptive of God than others. Sometimes the church came near to shipwreck on the rocks or power-hungry leaders with ambitions uninformed by Christ. Sometimes what was taught was wrong, as when churches argued for racism and apartheid. But sometimes, by the grace of God and the work of the Spirit there are times of renewal, new glimpses of the truth, as God, who never imposes his will and way, helps his disciples to see again and walk a different path. So we come to understand that the church is always in need of reformation, *semper reformanda*, not least because sometimes reformations have unintended results and because later generations have the ability to turn words of grace into demands of law.[7] The church's hope is always going to be in God, the God to whom the Scriptures and the ongoing story of the church bear witness.

In Scripture, we are bidden to love God with all our minds (Matt. 22:37; Mark 12:30; Luke 10:27). Thinking and speaking about God is part of the task of the church. We touched on this in Chapter 5. We have to learn the language of the faith, to speak Christian, as it were. We are told that the early Christians took years in preparing people for baptism, teaching them the story of Christ, teaching them not just the words but how to pray, how to live.[8] Theology, speaking and thinking about God, is not the task only of a special group of people in the church with academic interests. It is the calling of all members in Christ. We have come to believe that a profound weakness of the contemporary church in the western world is our assumption that we know what the words 'God', 'sin', 'grace', 'love' and 'hope' mean, and that we know the essential Christian story. But we doubt this, not least in what has happened to the great festival of the incarnation of the Son of God we call Christmas.

It is not that we need to learn as by rote the ancient ways and words. We need to hear again the biblical story and learn to think about it again as God speaks today. The history of the church is important because, honestly told, it has important warnings and strong indicators to help us. But that we need to become a new community of disciples, following Jesus, we have no doubt. It is urgent for our time because we have allowed other stories to dominate our minds; stories of nationalism, economic longing, violence and individual security. But the fact is that thinking about the things of God, experiencing the renewing of our minds has always been a necessary work of God for us – but for that we must think again, and again. 'Do not be conformed to this world, but be transformed by the renewing of your minds, so that you may discern what is the will of God – what is good and acceptable and perfect' (Rom. 12:2).[9]

Faith – Reason – Practice

When we assert our conviction that we need to learn to think Christianly we do not want to imply that Christian living is essentially an intellectual activity. What we are saying is that the gift of reasoning is from God who made us in God's own image. Faith and reason are inseparably related. This is not to say that being a Christian is first and foremost a great intellectual exercise so that only the really clever can be true Christians. That idea is offensive and unworthy, indicating a lack of understanding of the nature of faith in God. But for reasons of understanding and proclaiming the faith, trust and reason go together and are necessary for each other. We do not think that Christians had anything to fear from this approach, the engagement with deep questions of life. To the contrary, it was what we owe to God in worship and loving response to the divine gracious initiative.

However, we do not think that human reason is the first, let alone the last and final authority. As far as we are concerned it is God's love for us revealed in Jesus and our love of God rather than our knowledge of God that really matter. Christians should *think* about their faith and *for* their faith, as an act of devotion to God. Our thinking is part of our exploration of God's existence and being and so is one with our acts of searching prayer, alive and complete only in the context of worship. Faith and reason need each other and come as gifts of God. We search for the truth only to discover that we have been found by the truth discovering us. Thus reason, faith as trust, practising the virtues, offering prayer and worship all belong together in God. We affirm this vision of the whole world, of all that is, in existence and essence, before God. Wherever we find the living church we find people thinking, loving God with their minds, trying to understand their calling and the gifts of God. It is no surprise that the history of the church is, in some measure, the history of theology, of the different responses in different contexts to the gospel.

So, our argument has been that our knowledge of God comes from God's own initiative recorded in Scripture, especially Jesus, reflected on by the church from the first, with lived experience of God, through thought and reason. But there is one other feature of knowing God we wish to accentuate, one that is essential to the biblical account of knowledge of God: it is a matter of practice.

Let us take some biblical examples. In Jeremiah 22 there is a passage which announces judgement against the sons of Josiah. Josiah lived simply, keeping the covenant obligations of a faithful Israelite king. Thus, 'He judged the cause of the poor and needy; then it was well. Is not this to know me? says the Lord' (Jer. 22:16). By sad contrast his sons did not know the Lord, demonstrated in their disobedience and selfishness. So knowledge that does not lead to good covenant deeds is not knowledge at all. Likewise, Psalm 79:6, Exodus 5:2 and Hosea 8:1–3 all make the point that knowing and obeying God are allied if not identical activities. You cannot have one without the other. The only way to know God is to obey in our dealings with other people and the world in general, and in worship.

The same approach is taken in the New Testament. Indeed Jesus says, 'My teaching is not mine but his who sent me. Anyone who resolves to do the will of God will know whether the teaching is from God or whether I am speaking on my own' (John 7:16–17).

The person who really knows that Jesus has come from the Father is one who seeks to do the Father's will, following Jesus. Or take the case of Paul involved in a debate about knowledge: 'we know that "all of us possess knowledge." Knowledge puffs up, but love builds up. Anyone who claims to know something does not yet have the necessary knowledge; but anyone who loves God is known by him' (1 Cor. 8:1–3). Reflecting on the new commandment of God John sharply asserts, 'We love because he first loved us. Those who say "I love God", and hate their brothers or sisters, are liars; for those who do not love a brother or sister whom they have seen, cannot love God whom they have not seen. The commandment we have from him is this: those who love God must love their brothers and sisters also' (1 John 4:19–21). Treatment of the poor is a test case for Christian truthfulness in the letter of James (Jas 2:1–7).

And so we could go on. Knowing God is not just a matter of believing, even the devils do that (Jas 2:19). Neither can knowing God be reduced to enjoying certain kinds of religious experiences. Nothing short of a whole way of life before God is involved. Doctrine and practice, faith and ethics are inseparably related. We tell a different story in the church, one of God revealed in Jesus. Because of that story we live differently. Because of God and our relationship as creatures, made in God's image, revealed and enlivened by Jesus Christ, in the Spirit, we live responsively, sharing a divinely initiated partnership. So, the knowing of God is inseparable from doing the things of God. The knowing is the doing and the doing is the knowing.[10] All this is well said by Hans Denck, an early Anabaptist: 'No one can truly know [Christ] unless he follows him in life, and no one may follow him unless he has first known him.'[11]

Examples of Faith in Practice

It has been our argument, based on Scripture, that we are creatures, made in God's image and partners with God. 'The earth is the LORD's and all that is in it, the world, and those who live in it' (Ps. 24:1). This far-reaching radical view of life means we are not the owners of the earth to exploit it as we wish. Moreover, all those who live on the earth belong fundamentally to God. That is their worth and status. Believing these things about God has made and still makes for some challenging ways of life.

One significant example comes from the early Anabaptists as they wished to affirm the point just made about the significance of orthopraxis, the call to follow Jesus. At Schleitheim, Switzerland, in 1527, Anabaptists from various contexts worked at their disagreements and came to a consensus which they expressed in seven articles. It remains a challenging statement of the Christian way of life in the community of the church as well as being a statement of explanation to all readers. What is so striking is how simple, direct and practical it is.[12] The influence of the tradition of church life that had shaped the earlier lives of these radical believers is shown in their dating the document on St Matthew's Day, Anno MDXXVII.

What the confessions of the Reformation sought to do was to hold together the Bible, tradition and Spirit. They valued the tradition of the faith but not without questioning its affirmations and practices, bringing all to the test of Scripture. They enjoyed the freedom in the Spirit to be open to new gifts of God but they were aware of the dangers of a lack of discernment, oppressive leadership, and the seeming inevitability of schisms. It is a sorry feature of Protestantism that it shows itself to be so given to divisions. The kind of mutual accountability found at Schleitheim was not always present and arguments, power struggles and personality clashes challenged the convictions in Scripture of the 'one holy catholic and apostolic church'. Of course, you may believe that you and your group alone are right in doctrine and practice, the one true church on earth. This is a huge claim to make before God! Is such certainty that we are right and all else wrong not a temptation to spiritual arrogance and pride? Might we not ask with Paul in apostolic humility, 'Who has known the mind of the Lord?' (Rom. 11:33–6).

There are forms of Christian believing, statements claiming doctrinal purity and finality that are too confident to be true. When and if any Christian group tries to impose its teachings on others, denying the possibility of question or doubt, they have gone too far. Their god has become an idol they seek to impose on others. It is not Christian faith they are proclaiming. Such certainty in language is beyond us when it comes to God. It is no accident that the great creeds begin with *Credo* or *Credimus*, that is, 'I believe' or 'we believe'. They do not say, 'I know'. Yet the faith is knowledge, where 'I believe' carries more the sense of trust, of personal relations then just intellectual conviction. And the knowledge of God grows as our minds are remade and our natures transformed, but not without practice of the faith. Gospel truth is only known in experience, and experience is only developed in practice. This cannot be coerced or imposed.

For example, let us picture a congregation standing and affirming the creed: 'who for us, and our salvation, came down from heaven, and was incarnate by the Holy Spirit by the Virgin Mary and was made man'. They are affirming that Jesus, the Son of God, was fully a man, fully human, sharing the humanity – male and female – we all share, made in the image of God, accountable and responsible to God. Jesus is one with every person of every colour and tribe and nation. Although it has often taken the church a long time to see this and to live accordingly, it means that the kind of distinctions drawn among us to the inclusion of some and the exclusion of others have no place in the community gathered in the name and way of Jesus (Gal. 3:28).

Now, if you believe in the incarnation of the Son of God then how you treat people will be different from those who have another assessment of what it is to be a human being. For example, one Baptist church in London in 1851 placed an advertisement in *The Times* stating, in the face of the expected arrival of many Americans coming for the Great Exhibition, 'That this Church cannot admit to the fellowship of the Lord's table any person whatever, who either sympathises with or supports the Fugitive Slave Law of the United States; or who withholds his influence from the efforts which are being made for restoring to the coloured population of the United States the rights of which they have been so wickedly deprived.'[13] Behind this policy of discipline of rejecting racism was a theological conviction about incarnation. Orthodoxy without orthopraxis rings hollow.

Another illustration. On the plain white walls of Didsbury Baptist Church in Manchester, England, hangs one of those brightly decorated crosses from El Salvador. It was made in memory of Maria Christina Gomez who was a school teacher, active in a local church in San Salvador and a critic of the government's ruthless repression of human rights. In 1989 she was abducted, tortured and shot by the security forces. She was one of many ordinary Christians who – like El Salvador's martyr, Bishop Oscar Romero – suffered persecution and death because of their convictions about God.

The Beginning and the End is Worship

This means that there is always a necessary element of mystery for us before God. It is not that here we find a puzzle too great for our minds, as if God is the end of some great equation or formula. It is because God is mysterious, beyond us, unspeakable and encountered in the depths of silence, known to us only because God has spoken. Perhaps it is because there is something frightening in this thought that we have often resorted to reducing faith and worship to feel-good therapy sessions.

We are grateful to God for the self-revelation in Israel's story, in Jesus, recorded in the Scriptures. We are grateful also for the long history of Christian thought on these matters, exploring what it is to trust and live in the way of our Saviour. Faith to be faith must be free. It goes on in a world of remarkable discoveries, or the amazing growth in knowledge about the world of God's making. It is a sign of faith and trust in God that we try to hold all of this together, for it all belongs together, faith and science, belief and knowledge, tradition and Spirit, convictions and doubts, grief at our sin and gratitude for gracious forgiveness. Living with these tensions is loving God with our minds, but not our intellects only. The fear of the Lord is the beginning of knowledge (Prov. 1:7) so love the Lord your God with heart, soul, strength and mind and your neighbour as yourself. All this is involved in the knowing of the unknowable Holy God.

One important consequence of this is that theological reflections upon the Scriptures, the tradition of Christian thought, our lived experience of grief and glory, what else we know about ourselves and the world, all this is crucial for living faith and the life of the church before God! This Christians must do together. The declaring and proclaiming of the faith is a church task and needs all the insights of the whole church in its practice of discipleship. Any neglect of the past, any denigration of the intellect does no honour to God. That God, revealed in Scripture, known in Jesus, by the power of the Holy

Spirit, *is* good news. The maker and enabler of all that is, active even now in the sweep of history, patiently and lovingly working with us, bringing all things to conclusion without coercion or threat, this God of peace and love is worthy of worship. As Paul puts it:

> O the depth of the riches and wisdom and knowledge of God! How unsearchable are his judgements and how inscrutable his ways! 'For who has known the mind of the Lord? Or who has been his counsellor?' 'Or who has given a gift to him, to receive a gift in return?' For from him and through him and to him are all things. To him be the glory for ever. Amen. (Rom. 11:34–6).

PART THREE:

ENCOUNTERING GOD

7.

Experience of God

All-wise. All-powerful. All-loving. All-knowing.
We bore to death both God and ourselves with our chatter.
God cannot be expressed, only experienced.
— Frederick Buechner (b. 1926)[1]

What is Experience?

It seems obvious to record that how we experience life in this world has changed and with it our beliefs about the world. Our beliefs and experience of life are related. Changes in one sphere affect the other. Certainly the Lisbon earthquake we referred to in the introduction caused many people to reflect on their experience of life before God. We never simply have 'experience'. It is always experience of something or someone. The sum of our life may be called our experience of life but that broad brush stroke of description only cloaks the details, when what we believe changes because of what we experience and what we experience changes because of changes in convictions and ways of looking at the world, that is, our beliefs. The philosopher Karl Popper helpfully taught us that all experience is conceptually loaded and context-dependent. We do not have any 'experience' that is not conceptually 'made'.

> We do not stumble upon our experiences, nor do we let them flow over us like a stream. Rather, we have to be active: we have to '*make*' our experiences. It is we who always formulate the questions to put to nature; it is we who try again and again to put these questions so as to elicit a clear-cut 'yes' or 'no' (for nature does not give an answer

unless pressed for it). And in the end, it is again we who give the answer; it is we ourselves who, after severe scrutiny, decide upon the answer to the questions which we put to nature.[2]

Let us take 1 Samuel 3 as a biblical example. It is the story of the calling of the boy Samuel to be a prophet. It happened at a low point in Israel's faith journey. Eli, the priest, who with his sons was responsible for teaching Torah, the way of the covenant people to live, was not the perceptive man he had once been. Because the priests had not been teaching Torah, the religious life of the people was at a dangerously low ebb, although the light had not quite gone out (1 Sam. 3:3). The temple was little used. This was not Israel's most glorious age of faith. In the night Samuel hears his name being called. He goes to wake Eli up, assuming he is being summoned. Eli denies calling the boy and sends him back to bed. This happens twice more. We can imagine the growing irritation of the old man with this troublesome youth. The editor tells us that at the time Samuel did not know the Lord (1 Sam 3:7) but once more he hears the calling of his name. This time what little remained of Eli's sense of spiritual discernment and perception comes alive and he tells Samuel how to respond. In philosophical terms, he gives him the concept of the Lord calling. Only now is the boy able to interpret and enter into the experience of being called by God. Eli has this key role. Should he have failed, Samuel might well have grown up to tell his grandchildren how when he was a little boy he had to sleep in that ruined temple that no one ever goes to these days with an old man who talked in his sleep. What other explanation might there be? All experience is conceptually loaded and has its own context. Eli, living in the story that Samuel has yet to learn, gives the clue and sets the context. The stories that people live by are important for interpreting their lived experience.

Experiencing God Unawares?

So, might it be the case that many people in this generation do in fact have experiences of God but lack the language to identify and express their response? This might be because the understanding of the story changes. For example, at one time the exploding of a volcano, a violent destructive storm, a flood or an earthquake might have been interpreted as an act of God to which the only response was penitence and prayer because such had obviously come as the judgement of God – or so religious officials seeking to control a population might have taught. Nowadays we would say that such events were 'natural' disasters, the shifting of tectonic plates or changing weather systems. We do not think of these events as the work of God because we no longer see God as the cause and explanation of them. 'God', we have come to realize, is not an explanatory term at all, however much we might otherwise wish.

There seems to be something about our humanity, our shared experience that makes us wonder, not about explanations, but about what is going on in the human story and what it might mean. Here are some pictures of human experience, all of which suggest a depth to life we do not always acknowledge. One concerns a young woman who burst into a London church late one afternoon. She met the minister and asked if she could go into the sanctuary. She went right down to the front, before the table. She threw her arms into the air, then knelt, then prostrated herself, only to stand with arms outstretched again. This went on for about fifteen minutes until she came out of the door. The minister asked if she was all right. 'All right!' she responded. 'It's better than all right. You see, I am an actress and I have just got my first part on a West End stage. I had to come and say "thank you" to someone.' She did not identify to whom the gratitude was expressed. For her, this was a moment of wonder and joy and that was what she was recognizing.

Something not dissimilar happens when a father or mother has the new baby placed in their arms. Some parents become speechless, overwhelmed by the emotion of the moment of gratitude and wonder. They are 'in touch' with something sacred. Something similar can happen in a concert hall when an audience is captivated and moved by the music, responding with a silence only reluctantly broken in applause.

Or take the recent film *Philomena* which tells a story full of emotion and depth. It begins in Ireland in the early 1950s.[3] A young unmarried woman conceives a child out of wedlock. In the film she talks of the illicit sex as being a beautiful experience and wonders how anyone could think of it, as the nuns taught her, as sin. As was not uncommon in those days, in disgrace, she went to a home for unmarried mothers to work while the nuns cared for the child. It transpires in the film that the nuns 'sold on' these children to Americans without any discussion with the parents, except they signed away their rights to any future meeting with their children. Philomena's son went to America where he grew to be very successful. He was homosexual, and before his early death came back to Ireland to seek his mother. He was told by the sisters that they had no information, even that his mother was probably dead. Philomena had been told the same when in later years she had sought to find out about her son. It is a deeply moving film and it is not unknown for the audience audibly to respond at the portrayal of the callousness of the sisters, still insisting on the guilt of the wicked sinner in their charge, and then to fall silent as Philomena says she forgives those who did her such hurt and harm. The journalist travelling with Philomena states categorically that he cannot forgive what the nuns have done. But then in the film we have already learned that Philomena believes in God and the journalist does not.

The story is not unique, of course, and the questions it raises are fundamental to us as human beings. There are different interpretations of 'right' and 'wrong', of what it is to be loving and human. Issues of power and the meaning of forgiveness are at stake. Such things are common to our being human, part of our experience; but how shall we interpret them? Could these be experiences of God which we miss either because we do not think of God or because our thoughts are theologically misleading? Is it possible that we can have an experience of God but miss the meaning because we do not know the language, like Samuel, or because the language has gone dead on us and no longer 'speaks'?

Let us return to the Bible where, as we have argued earlier, there are no philosophical arguments for the existence of God but rather God is just 'there', given, fundamental. Everything that is, is before God, exists in God and is acted upon by God. 'God' is not introduced to explain or justify but simply is before all time, the One in whom all things live and move and have their being (Acts 17:28). Given this perspective on all life we might expect stories of particular experiences of God as well as recognizing ways by which life is understood before God. So, for example, the book of Psalms gives expression to life in various moods before God. There is wonder and amazement at the thought that in such a vast universe God should be mindful of humankind (Ps. 8). Since life does not always go well there are cries to God for help and deliverance, a recognition of who ultimately matters (Pss 12 and 13). Life before God is not to be taken for granted, especially when it comes to worship (Ps. 15). In contexts where life is uncertain and insecure then the overcoming of a grave illness, or of safety in a storm, become occasions of prayer and praise (Pss 29 and 30). There is the experience of longing for a deeper sense of God (Ps. 42), of the utter trustworthiness of God before the machinations of the nations (Ps. 46), of the good news of the inescapability of God (Ps. 139). And so we could go on. All human life is here, life before God.

Stories in the Bible

Sometimes this shows itself in particular lives and moments. We have already referred to the call of Samuel. The story of Moses has two formative experiences in close proximity. One is, for all his upbringing in Pharaoh's court, the sense of injustice as he sees an Egyptian beating a Hebrew slave. Moses cannot let this pass so he up and kills the Egyptian, an incident that causes him to flee for safety to a foreign land. But then, while working as a herdsman for his new father-in-law, he sees a bush that burns but is not consumed. He draws near only to find himself addressed. He is on holy ground. He is not engaged in any cultic activity. He is called by God, the God who also has heard the cry of the oppressed people. Moses is called into partnership with God to set the people free (Exod. 2 – 3).

Another call story is in Isaiah 6. It is set in a time of political crisis and uncertainty. Uzziah the king is dead and now what will happen? Isaiah lives in Jerusalem, possibly as a member of the royal court, so he would be caught up in the political speculation about who would come to reign now there is a vacancy. He goes to the place of worship and is given an amazing experience of God, of the One who reigns whoever is king in Jerusalem. Isaiah recognizes his own unworthiness but hears the call of God.

A New Testament illustration concerns Saul of Tarsus. He was a zealous Jew, a Pharisee of the Pharisees, and a serious opponent of the new group who claimed that the Messiah had come and that his name was Jesus (Phil. 3:4–6). Saul was authorized to stamp out this aberration and he stood witness as a crowd stoned Stephen to death (Acts 7:54 – 8:1). He then set off for Damascus to rid that city of the sectarian disease. On the road he was met by the risen Christ who called him to missionary service, essentially to proclaim Jesus as the Christ, saviour of Jews and Gentiles.

Stories Outside the Bible

These are three spectacular stories from the Bible of direct experiences of God. Such stories are not confined to the Bible. They are part of the ongoing story of the church. So, for example, Augustine (354–430), the brilliant debater acknowledges an emptiness in his life. Self-examination could reduce him to tears but he tells of a moment when he hears a voice from a house nearby, saying over and over again, 'Take and read, take and read.' He goes indoors and takes up his copy of the Bible, turning randomly to Romans: 'Let us live honourably as in the day, not in revelling and drunkenness, not in debauchery and licentiousness, not in quarrelling and jealousy. Instead, put on the Lord Jesus Christ, and make no provision for the flesh, to gratify its desires' (Rom. 13:13–14). He became a Christian with his doubts overcome.[4] This is but one part of his lived experience but it was transformative of his life.

The story of John Wesley's conversion is well known, with his heart being strangely warmed, as he records in his journal.[5] What is less well known is the story of the very influential American Methodist Phoebe Palmer (1807–74). Married to a doctor she had six children, only three of whom survived beyond childhood. One child died in tragic circumstances leaving Palmer in deep grief. She turned to the Bible and in her own words:

> While pacing the room, crying to God, amid the tumult of grief, my mind was arrested by a gentle whisper, saying, 'Your heavenly Father

loves you. He would not permit such a great trial, without intending that some great good proportionate in magnitude and weight should result... In the agony of my soul I had exclaimed, 'O, what shall I do?' and the answer came, 'Be still and know that I am God.'[6]

In nineteenth century when women were not often in positions of leadership and authority Palmer went on to have huge influence in the holiness tradition, driven as she was by her experience of God.

By no means does every Christian have such overwhelming ecstatic experiences of the Spirit, although this may happen more than we realize since such events are not easily spoken about. But it is certainly a long tradition we are touching upon here, one that is far from over. Of course, there is a difference from claiming to have an experience of God and actually encountering God. People have claimed to have heard God speaking to them only later to find that was not the case. Sometimes the emotive effect of acts of worship can be taken for a genuine encounter with God, a feeling that quickly dissipates on leaving the building. But having said that it cannot be denied how often such claims to 'meet' God arise, how widespread in the human story are the claims to such living experiences. This would come as no surprise if the Christian claim that we are all made in the image of God were true. We might expect the 'capacity for God' to be a feature of what it is to be human. We might also note that many of those who speak of an encounter with God show the truth of that in the changed ways of life they live.

Analyzing Experience of God

One of the most helpful analyses of religious experience was made by the British theologian Herbert Henry Farmer (1892–1981).[7] He argued that we often misread the world in which we live because we think of it and study it in detachment from ourselves. Impersonal philosophies of life dominate and shape our experience but if we are to take seriously our experience of the world as a whole then it must include ourselves, we who have wills to exercise and minds to decide. Not least, our experience of the world includes that of other persons who have wills and desires of their own which may be co-operative with or in opposition to our own. Such matters cannot be fully appreciated by examination in detachment in a laboratory. Another kind of personal engagement is necessary, a deeper examination of the psychological and logical nature of our experience.

After careful examination, Farmer concluded that there are three interrelated elements in religious experience, or experience of God. One is something that happens in the sphere of our wills. In everyday as well as particularly religious contexts such as worship, we can find ourselves encountered by another will, so strong that it is unconditional in its demand, even to the cost of life itself. We cannot lay such an unconditional claim upon ourselves. Such an experience does not vary according to mood or desire. It is just there, some right thing we must do, some wrong thing we must avoid, unconditionally. This, argues Farmer, is the claim of God. It is not that we deduce from the experience that it is so strong it must be of God, as if God is the explanation of what is happening. Rather the experience of unconditional demand is the awareness of God as personal will, addressing and claiming my will. God is not evoked as an attempt to make sense of this absolute resistance to my will. Rather such an experience is the experience of God, an experience like no other.

Second and inseparably related to that sense of absolute demand is the awareness of final security. It is God's claim, the foundation of the world of values, a claim to be trusted and obeyed, because it is the claim of God. This is why in God's service there is perfect freedom or, as Jesus said, 'Those who want to save their life will lose it, and those who lose their life for my sake, and for the sake of the gospel, will save it' (Mark 8:35). This is why some martyrs in their dying seem more alive than their killers. It may seem very unsettling to fall into the hands of the living God, to meet his unconditional demand, but we are in the saving safe hands of God. In God's will is our peace. It is why there is a long tradition, from Peter and Paul to Bonhoeffer, that could write about and celebrate freedom while in a prison cell. Bonhoeffer was the free man in the service of God. It was his jailers who were bound.[8]

So the experience of unconditional demand and of ultimate safety are part of living experience *of God*. Part but not the whole.

Farmer claims the experience, the feeling, is like no other because it is experience of God. That is what makes it like no other. That is why traditionally Christians have spoken of awe before God, a deep unsought and uncreatable feeling given as God draws near.[9] Because this is the experience of God it is both like and unlike our experience of meeting other wills in the forms of other human beings. The experience of God, however, is unique so that in the nature of the case there can be no analogies. As Farmer argues:

> We would expect that if we know the reality of God in respect of this fundamental aspect of his [sic] being at all, we shall just know it, and we shall just know we are dealing with God, the ultimate source and disposer of all things, including ourselves, and there will be nothing more to be said. It will not be possible to describe the compelling touch of God otherwise than as the compelling touch of God.[10]

We have argued earlier in this book that Christians must attend carefully to the language they use. This is why the language of the tradition is so important. Of course, language changes in its use and therefore in its meaning. Take, for example, the word 'awe'. It has a new recent widespread use by a younger generation who express their pleasure at something they enjoy by describing it as 'awesome', which in the jargon might also be described as 'cool'. So a new pair of jeans, or a film, or a new song learned at a conference may be 'awesome'. The word expresses delight, pleasure, approval and joy. It is a word naturally used by Christian young people who have shared the worship of a big conference they have attended. In those terms it may have to do with God.

Farmer would expect that if it were a genuine experience of God then it would lead to differences in living and relating to others. There has been a tendency in much contemporary Christianity to emphasize the nearness, the warmth, the closeness of God our best friend. However, the tradition of the faith, while never denying this nearness of God speaks also of God's otherness, distance, awe-fullness. 'It is a fearful thing to fall into the hands of the living God' (Heb. 10:31). Here is another sense of awe that the tradition of the faith keeps alive and that is important, lest we start to recreate in language a less than truthful picture of God.

We have emphasized in the recent paragraphs the directness of some religious experiences, moments of encounter and calling. This way of speaking of God has been particularly marked in the evangelical, charismatic, Pentecostal and holiness traditions of the Christian faith although it is hardly contained there alone. It is a feature of such Pentecostal and other traditions that each believer should be able to testify to some special moments of encounter with God, which is taken to be essential to the faith. As we have indicated, this understanding of experience of God has a long history from biblical times onward. It has been characteristic of some of the most inspiring witnesses to the living God in the church and world. We live in hope that by the active Spirit of God such encounters will continue to happen.

However, that is not the whole story of God's ways with us. There are many faithful disciples who have never had such an intensity of personal call but who none the less trust the love and life of the Triune God and look to live their lives in response to the gospel of Jesus Christ. They have come to trust the apostolic message and live their lives in the light of the message of divine love and grace. The contrast between these two approaches can be put this way. Some, in the midst of their everyday living, often unexpectedly find themselves surprisingly addressed by God. Others, while never having had such surprises live all their days before God, in faith and trust and so experience all life differently from that of an unbeliever. The religious experience of such people is their experience of life before God. They do not think that God can ever be relegated to certain experiences, even to a realm called 'religion' alone, as if that were the special interest of God. Rather, religious experience is that of a seriously religious person, one who holds the thought of God before their minds and so experiences everything in life before God. Holding such a conviction means that although the believer and unbeliever can go through the same events in life they experience them differently.

This takes us back to the point we made earlier about all experience being conceptually loaded, of how God is understood and conceived. Different 'pictures' of God can lead to different experiences of God, different ways of seeing and living life. We have already emphasized the importance of the doctrine of the Trinity for Christian life and thought. Supposing we did not think of God in that way but rather drew a severe distinction between the Father and the Son, then we might be left with an erroneous picture of a father who was prepared to have his son killed for the father's own satisfaction.[11] Would such a father be worthy of worship? Would such a father evoke love or fear? Such a distinction between Father and Son is not part of the doctrine of God in Trinity where relationships of love dominate and liberate. We always need to tell the old, old story carefully lest we distort the vision of God. It is not difficult to see how other ways of speaking of God can lead to different experiences and ways of life. Here are three illustrations.

Beginning in the third century there emerged new buildings in which the growing church could meet. Instead of meeting in homes the church now had big basilicas in which to gather, appropriate to their new social standing. These buildings made a statement and they required professional leadership to make them work. The models for church architects were the secular buildings of imperial Rome. And the professionals, priests and bishops, saw how the clothing and status of politicians set them apart and started to copy them, wearing garments that suggested who was in charge there. Of course, there was language in the Scriptures of kings and monarchs that encouraged this. But the overall effect of this was to drive a new wedge into the church, between ordained and laity, and to suggest that the most appropriate pictures of God were of majesty, kingship, power and authority. Inevitably, perhaps, these were modelled on the emperors and monarchs of the day. The laity obeyed the bishops and the people obeyed their king. While such pictures may find some support in the Bible they are far from the whole truth of the God who shares the life of the vulnerable and poor and washes the feet of the needy, whose presence among us is as one who serves, who has nowhere on which to lay his head. Secular models of kingship did not always have a good effect on the developing life of the church, and we saw this already in the biblical witness. This was an unfortunate aspect of the times but while the church remained open to the Scriptures and the tradition the resources were there for God to lead the church in other more Christlike ways. That happened!

Second, a contrast is sometimes drawn by Christian thinkers between what they call *theologia gloriae* and *theologia crucis*. Of course the church wants to praise and glorify God for all that God has done in creation and redemption. We have a song to sing and words of praise to utter. *Theologia gloriae* is this celebration of God as we join our voices and sing, 'Holy, holy, holy Lord, heaven and earth are full of thy glory!' However, such an emphasis to the exclusion of all others can lead not to the proper joy in God's work but to triumphalism. It happens when faith becomes an ideology with which to conquer all the peoples of the world. The church triumphant looks to control others, to have their obedience because God has shared his glory with us and only us. What is forgotten or ignored is the costly calling to discipleship for the world in the name of the God who knows the suffering and sacrifice of the cross, *theologia crucis*. Such an approach really does believe that the fullest expression of God's love for the world is to be seen in the cross of Jesus Christ. *Theologia crucis* is first of all a statement about God, our crucified God, whose glory is seen in the face of Jesus Christ (2 Cor. 4:6).[12] Such an understanding of God calls into question any enthusiasms for theologies of prosperity in which faithfulness to God results in personal prosperity, health and wealth. Since God is revealed in Jesus of the cross and resurrection then all genuine experience of God will include both a bearing of the cross and the sharing of Christ's sufferings as well as joy in the resurrection life (Phil. 3:10).

As a third illustration, let us recall something of what we said earlier of our speaking about God. As people increasingly sought explanations for what was happening in the world and their own lives from the eighteenth century onwards, so they resorted less and less to the thought of God as an explanation. Once everything that took place had been attributed to God's action, or so it was believed. We have an illustration of this in an incident involving the town of Warminster in Wiltshire, England, in 1866. The vicar wrote his parishioners a letter from his holiday villa in Italy expressing his delight that the 'Days of Humiliation for the cattle plague were so well observed'.[13] We know the cattle plague today as foot-and-mouth disease and upon its outbreak we would first call upon veterinary surgeons and government farming officials for help, before ever turning to God in the conviction that this disaster had come upon us because of sins of which we needed to repent in deep humiliation.

A lot has happened in our experience and understanding in the last two hundred years. Today we first think that a change in the weather is due to climate forces. Quite possibly, as weather systems sweep towards us, we do not pray for good weather at the church fete. Instead we might even take out insurance against the whole event being rained off. The insurance company could even call such an eventuality 'an act of God'. They identify God as a cause, an explanation, as did the vicar of Warminster.

But is God an 'explanation', to be invoked as a member of a class of possible explanations, an alternative to the weather systems we identify? Those who thought, or think, like this are basically invoking a god which is another name for what we do not know, a god which is a gap in our knowledge, a cause that could never be identified. If this the way we think of God then we shall find, as we have already found, that the 'places' for God become smaller and smaller, increasingly private, as we live by other explanations of life and experience. Thus it is that more and more people have come to live without the thought of God at all, without that explanatory hypothesis. Could it be that this increasingly describes the state of some present-day churches? But as we have asserted from the beginning of this book, God is not like this at all and to have faith in God is quite different from holding a hypothesis in our minds.

By contrast, it has been our argument that the thought of God is not reduced to being an explanation. In fact, we are wanting to support the earlier approach of the church that affirmed the presence of God in all life and all things living in God. Psalm 150:6 calls on everything that breathes to praise the Lord! Psalm 145:10 declares that all God's works shall give thanks to the Lord. The meaning of all this is found in doxology, in the praise of God. This must include the light and the darkness of life. God is unique, not a member of any class we can think of or desire. There is a mystery about God that is not the experience of being mystified and puzzled but goes deeper than that.

8.

God and Evil

And I heard a great voice out of heaven saying, Behold, the tabernacle of God is with men, and he will dwell with them, and they shall be his people, and God himself shall be with them, and be their God. And God shall wipe away all tears from their eyes; and there shall be no more death, neither sorrow, nor crying, neither shall there be any more pain: for the former things are passed away. And he that sat upon the throne said, Behold, I make all things new.

– Revelation 21:3–5 (KJV)

Facing Evil

The question of how we can reconcile the bare facts of the existence of evil in the world with a loving and omnipotent God who acts in history is among the most potent and contested questions of our day. In the wake of events of great destruction, whether of the natural or moral kind, a veritable cacophony of voices bursts forth to announce whatever greater significance they perceive in the event in question. Among these voices we are by now accustomed to hearing the triumphant atheist pronounce (again) that here at last we have an instance of horror on so terrifyingly vast a scale that we can no longer countenance belief in a loving and omnipotent God. Despite the increasing volume of the atheist voice in our day, we shall be more concerned in this chapter to examine what we think is the more troubling question of the extent to which Christian theology itself has recently begun to agree with its atheist counterparts on the question of evil and suffering.[1] Not, of course, on the basic question of the existence or non-existence of God but rather on the assumption that the twentieth century has brought forth evil on such a scale that the traditional Christian thinking about God must be called into question and, at least for the theologians, ultimately reformulated if it is to have any contemporary relevance. There is a curious and troubling trend within Christianity of all stripes that the doctrine of God as it has developed over centuries is simply no longer fit for purpose with respect to the question of evil. It is our conviction, however, that this trend rests on rather dubious caricatures of the tradition and that if we look a little bit deeper we will find a rich trove of resources for Christian living.

From Augustine to Auschwitz

For our purposes, we can helpfully see that the Christian tradition of thinking about evil is bound up with its thought about God by returning to Augustine's *Confessions*. In Chapter 5 we saw that Augustine came to a new conception of God as 'utterly different' and could not be thought of as a Being among beings. The fundamental distinction between creator and creatures in which all our speech about God is necessarily situated is also the context in which Augustine suggests we must think about evil. The reason Augustine gives for this is quite clear and comes directly on the heels of his realization that God is not a Being among beings: Because God has made all things very good (Gen. 1:31) everything that exists is good and therefore evil is not something that exists at all and can therefore only be thought of as a lack of good.[2]

Throughout his *Confessions*, Augustine is perennially concerned with the problem of evil, though he formulates this in a way that may strike contemporary readers as strange because it does not resemble the more fashionable theodicies to which we are more accustomed. Looking back on his childhood, he notes that he was 'so tiny a child, so great a sinner' primarily because he had no love for reading books, had to be forced to study and learned nothing of his own volition.[3] While we might balk at this as a rather quaint instance of 'evil', and perhaps something that is all too common today, what Augustine is getting at is that evil itself is pointless. Reflecting on why he disobeyed his parents and teachers, he says that he did so not because he had actively chosen to do something else with his time but rather out of competitiveness directed at winning empty victories.[4] The sheer pointlessness of evil is brought to the fore when Augustine famously describes the occasion when he and some friends stole some rather unattractive and tasteless pears from a neighbour's orchard. Their desire, as Augustine tells us, was not to enjoy the pears but merely to experience 'the excitement of thieving and the doing of what was wrong'.[5] The problem that gripped Augustine was that evil was indeed a powerful force but, in the end, was so utterly pointless that it amounted to nothing in and of itself.[6] So although Augustine maintains that evil is a lack of good, he is certainly not naive about the terrible positive consequences such an absence of good may have on concrete creaturely situations.

One way to understand what Augustine is trying to do is to highlight the sense in which talk about evil, like talk about God, must be 'de-spatialized'.[7] Evil, like God, has no *place* in the world. Likewise, neither evil nor God simply exist as creatures do, competing with others. When we talk about evil, then, we are not talking about some creaturely entity, physical or otherwise, that must be held back, controlled, manipulated or overcome. Rather when we talk about evil we are talking about the processes in which good is lost, processes in which we learn to see corruption. Throughout the *Confessions*, Augustine uses the metaphor of vision to describe the obfuscating effects of evil. He speaks of the mind's eye being clouded with images, somehow cut off from the divine light that is attempting to break forth, and opaque even to itself.[8] In his search for the origin of evil he says that God's healing touch had the effect of reducing the swelling that obscured his vision and allowed him to see that evil was not in a *place* and occupied no *space*.[9] In coming to this realization, Augustine finally sees that his quest for the origin of evil in the first place was flawed because he was looking for it among the created order and was therefore doomed to be frustrated.[10] His mistake was to try and understand the source and character of evil without placing this search in the context of God who alone is able to transfigure our desires and heal our blindness. As we will see, this mistake continues to be endemic to our thinking about evil.

The long tradition of thinking about evil as a lack of goodness wasn't given a good run for its money until around the seventeenth century when the God Augustine spoke of was emptied of transcendence and became instead the 'God of the philosophers'.[11] We might say that this is the historical moment at which the problem of evil as articulated by the pre-modern theologians became the problem of theodicy as articulated by the philosophers of 'enlightenment'. The term 'theodicy', which literally means a justification of God, was coined by Gottfried Leibniz who confidently declared that our world is the best of all possible worlds. Voltaire's poem with which we began our Introduction, written in the aftermath of the Lisbon earthquake, was a direct attack on what he saw as Leibniz's blithe confidence in the goodness of God in the face of a world shaken so violently to its knees. How could a world that unleashed such elemental violence and suffering be the best of all possible worlds? How are we to reconcile God's omnipotence, omniscience and benevolence with the existence and magnitude of evil on such a scale?

Not long after the quake, Immanuel Kant used the expression 'radical evil' to describe what he thought was an innate human propensity for evil.[12] Ever since Kant, there has been a fascination with this term, not least because some believe that Kant himself was only dimly aware of a kind of evil that exceeded the traditional Christian conceptions. Indeed, the twentieth century has borne witness to horrendous events that we desperately attempt to understand and to which we shall never be able to reconcile ourselves. Though we might mention any number of such events, 'Auschwitz' has become the name that epitomizes the Holocaust and stands as a terrifying symbol of evil that had hitherto been unthinkable. Hannah Arendt can be thought to speak for many when she described her shock when she first discovered what was taking place in the Nazi death camps:

> It was really as if an abyss had opened . . . *This ought not to have happened*. And I don't mean just the number of victims. I mean the method, the fabrication of corpses and so on – I don't need to go into that. This should not have happened. Something happened there, to which we cannot reconcile ourselves. None of us ever can.[13]

Despite the sustained intensity with which the events that unfolded in the Holocaust have been studied, Arendt's shock is no less forceful today than it was in 1942 when she first heard rumours about the extermination camps. Hitler's 'Final Solution' was an event whose very existence called life itself into question because it was the most radical form of genocide ever encountered: the wilful, systematic and industrially organized extermination of an entire group of people. Whatever slim layer of solidarity that had previously bound humanity together seemed to be wiped away for ever in the death camps.

In the face of this 'radical evil' it was abundantly clear that theology could not simply go on as usual; it now needed to be done in the light of 'Auschwitz'. Jürgen Moltmann sums up this deeply held intuition by arguing that:

> A theology after Auschwitz would be impossible, were not the *sch'ma* of Israel and the Lord's prayer prayed in Auschwitz itself, were not God himself in Auschwitz, suffering with the martyred and the murdered. Every other answer would be blasphemy. An absolute God would make us indifferent. The God of action and success would make us forget the dead, which we still cannot forget.[14]

For a host of modern theologians it is vital that our talk about God faces up to an unimaginable intensity of evil that has wrought terrible effects in the recent bloody theatre of history. The suffering of the modern era seems to demand new ways of speaking about God that are less beholden to what seem like the dogmatic complexities and philosophical abstractions that occupied the minds of the Fathers and the scholastics alike. In short, what seems to be required is a radical re-conception of the God who is not a Being among beings. The basic underlying intuition is that by living in solidarity with the wretched of the earth we are thereby living in solidarity with the suffering Christ who represents God in the world. Dorothee Sölle puts it this way: Christ 'suffers everything which results from the destruction of hope. The Lamb of God who "bears" the sin of the world is the man of God who "bears" the world's inhumanity.'[15]

Given the attempt to speak of the God who suffers with his creatures, it is not surprising that most of these attempts take the crucifixion as their primary point of departure. Moltmann argues that the passion of Christ, specifically Jesus' cry of Godforsakenness (Mark 15:34) on the cross, must be the starting point for theology.[16] In the light of the horrors of Auschwitz, he puts the matter forcefully by suggesting that 'to speak here of a God who could not suffer would make God a demon. To speak here of an absolute God would make God an annihilating nothingness. To speak here of an indifferent God would condemn men [sic] to indifference.'[17] The need to articulate a God who suffers with us is succinctly expressed by Dietrich Bonhoeffer, who was hanged in the Flossenbürg concentration camp just two weeks before it was liberated, when he said that 'only the suffering God can help'.[18]

Helpfully expanding the point of reference beyond 'Auschwitz' and confronting us with the ongoing realities of suffering, Gustavo Gutiérrez suggests that:

> Our task is to find the words with which to talk about God in the midst of the starvation of millions, the humiliation of races regarded as inferior, discrimination against women, especially women who are poor, systematic social injustice, a persistent rate of high infant mortality, those who simply 'disappear' or are deprived of their freedom, the sufferings of peoples who are struggling for their right to live, the exiles and the refugees, terrorism of every kind, and the corpse-filled common graves of Ayacucho [a scene of civil strife in Peru].[19]

Though all of these theologians articulate and defend their positions differently, they share a common goal to affirm that God shares in the suffering of his creatures through the incarnation and is thereby the agent of healing and hope in the world.

Does God Suffer?

That the contemporary experience of horrendous evil and suffering seems to necessitate a radical re-conception of the God who is not a Being among beings also apparently finds a strong warrant in the scriptural revelation of God. Indeed, throughout the biblical witness God is portrayed as a personal God who understands the plight of his people and acts decisively to save them. He not only made the heavens and the earth but also heard the cry of his people enslaved in Egypt and determined to rescue them from their suffering (Exod. 2:23–5; 3:7–8). This same God made covenants with his people, binding them to himself (Gen. 17; Exod. 24; Lev. 26:12; Jer. 11:4). The nearness with which this God draws to his people is affirmed again and again:

> Has any people ever heard the voice of a god speaking out of a fire, as you have heard, and lived? Or has any god ever attempted to go and take a nation for himself from the midst of another nation, by trials, by signs and wonders, by war, by a mighty hand and an outstretched arm, and by terrifying displays of power, as the LORD your God did for you in Egypt before your very eyes? (Deut. 4:33–4)

What is powerfully on display here is, quite simply, the covenant-love of God (Deut. 4:37). God is revealed again and again to be the God of compassion and love (Exod. 34:6–7; Isa. 63:7–9). The psalms too declare that God is a God who delivers his people in times of distress, a God who acts, forgives, heals and, above all, redeems life itself with steadfast love and mercy (Pss 18; 30; 40; 59; 66; 103; 119).

Even more than this, the prophets reveal God to be a God who grieves over the rebellion and unfaithfulness of his people. In Hosea, for example, God is distressed because even though he loved Israel from childhood they kept sacrificing to idols. Despite God leading them 'with cords of human kindness, with bands of love' violence raged in their cities because of their schemes that turned away from God (Hos. 11:1–7). God was so disheartened by this he became angry yet God could not hand Israel over because his 'compassion grows warm and tender': 'I will not execute my fierce anger; I will not again destroy Ephraim; for I am God and no mortal, the Holy One in your midst, and I will not come in wrath' (Hos. 11:8–9). This same dynamic of love overcoming God's anger is evident in Jeremiah: 'Is Ephraim my dear son? Is he the child I delight in? As often as I speak against him, I still remember him. Therefore I am deeply moved for him; I will surely have mercy on him, says the LORD' (Jer. 31:20).

Furthermore, there are numerous passages in the Old Testament that speak of God himself repenting of what he had intended to do, moved to pity and sometimes even changing his mind (Gen. 6:6–7; Exod. 32:11–14; Judg. 2:18; 1 Sam. 15:11; 2 Sam. 24:16; Jer. 18:8; Amos 7:1–6). These passages in the Old Testament seem to describe the 'sorrowing heart of God', what Paul Fiddes calls 'a blend of love and wrath . . . that is presented as a pathos which is God's own pathos'.[20]

The inescapable conclusion seems to be that for the claim 'God is love' (1 John 4:8) to have any recognizable continuity with our own experience, 'a loving God must be a sympathetic and therefore suffering God'.[21] Indeed, these arguments follow a very compelling pattern: if God is loving and if this God of love acts in history and is engaged with the lives of human beings, then such a God must also be capable of suffering. While the Old Testament surely lays the groundwork for this conception of God, it is the New Testament's proclamation that God became flesh and dwelt among us (John 1:14) that represents the most powerful claim that God suffers with all of creation because in the incarnation God becomes human, lives a fully human life and is executed as a political criminal. The cross becomes the paradigmatic example of the God who suffers: 'When the crucified Jesus is called the "image of the invisible God," the meaning is that *this* is God, and God is like *this* . . . The nucleus of everything that Christian theology says about "God" is to be found in this Christ event.'[22] Moltmann centres his analysis around Jesus' cry of dereliction on the cross (Mark 15:34): 'In the passion of the Son, the Father himself suffers the pains of abandonment. In the death of the Son, death comes upon God himself, and the Father suffers the death of his Son in his love for forsaken man [sic].'[23] For our purposes, what is most important here is the underlying assumption that the God who saves is the God who is incarnate in creation and is obedient unto death (Phil. 2:8). The crux of the matter, as Moltmann famously puts it, is that 'were God incapable of suffering in any respect . . . then he would also be incapable of love'.[24]

Challenging the Suffering God

Why labour this point, then? If God is not simply a bystander who stands aloof from creation while it suffers, if God is truly loving and compassionate then God too must suffer with creation. All this seems, at least on the surface, straightforward enough. However, the tradition of Christian thinking on this matter, inherited from the Fathers and the scholastics, held that God suffered in the incarnation only in the humanity of Jesus and not in his divine nature. The classical Christology of the Councils of Ephesus (431) and Chalcedon (451) developed the seemingly paradoxical idea that there is only one subject – the incarnate Word – but when we say that the Son was crucified we are saying that he suffered only according to his human nature and not according to his divine nature.

Fortunately, we need not go into great detail here for our purposes because what is most important to see is the massive shift that has occurred in a relatively short period of time. While the Fathers and the scholastics alike held that because the divine nature was impassible God could not suffer, contemporary theological reflection maintains, nearly in unison, that God can and does suffer.[25] The contrast is particularly stark if we compare the reflections of the modern theologians who advocate for a suffering God, as seen above, with Cyril of Alexandria (376–444) who states quite plainly that: 'God's word is, of course, undoubtedly impassible in his own nature and nobody is so mad as to imagine the all-transcending nature capable of suffering; but by very reason of the fact that he has become man, making flesh from the Holy Virgin his own, we adhere to the principles of the divine plan and maintain that he who as God transcends suffering, suffered humanly in his flesh.'[26] What are we to make of this radical shift? Has modern theology gone mad, as Cyril's reflection seems to imply? On the other hand, are we able to make any sense of the paradoxical notion that 'the impassible suffers?'[27]

The contemporary debates continue to rage here and we shall not do more than scratch the surface. Fortuitously for our purposes, we need not declare ourselves to be on one side or other of the ongoing passibility/impassibility debate.[28] The great value of the challenges that are brought to bear on the 'new orthodoxy' of the suffering God, whether we agree with them or not, lie in the fact that they oblige us to return again to the difficult question of God. What is implied about the character of God and on what basis are these arguments advanced? Does a God who is a 'fellow sufferer who understands' really help?[29] Critically reflecting on this contemporary conundrum, Karl Rahner suggests that:

> it does not help me to escape from my mess and mix-up and despair if God is in the same predicament. From the beginning I am locked into its horribleness while God – if this word continues to have any meaning – is in a true and authentic and consoling sense the God who does not suffer, the immutable.[30]

The problem that Rahner's reflection presses upon us is this: if God is God in and through the suffering of the cross, how is this grief-stricken and victimized God able to reconcile all of creation? In a sense, then, we are back to Augustine's problem: how can we speak of God who is revealed to us most explicitly in the life of Jesus Christ without speaking of God in a way that creates God in our own image? If we take our cue from Augustine, we must learn to avoid the same mistake he originally made by placing all our talk about evil and suffering in the context of God who alone is able to transfigure our desires and heal our blindness.

This is by no means a straightforward process. Indeed, at least part of the contemporary picture of a suffering God attempts to do just this by pointing out that an impassible God is, by definition, an apathetic and uncaring God who is unconcerned with the world and emotionally withdrawn. Thus advocates of a suffering God proceed on the basis of a critique of what they perceive to be a picture of God utterly incompatible with biblical revelation.[31] Admittedly, there are certainly multiple examples of what seem like highly infelicitous phrases that would make contemporary readers wonder if pre-modern theologians had wrestled seriously enough with Scripture.

Anselm of Canterbury's (1033–1109) explanation about how God can be both merciful and impassible is one such instance. Anselm concedes that 'if You are impassible You do not have any compassion; and if You have no compassion Your heart is not sorrowful from compassion with the sorrowful, which is what being merciful is'.[32] Though he goes on to explain that God can be both impassible and merciful because we feel the effects of

God's mercy, it can seem as though Anselm's desire to defend God's impassibility is driven primarily by philosophical considerations that can be held only at the expense of contradicting the biblical witness. This line of reasoning, however, is simply yet another instance of the genetic fallacy. For it to be true, we would need to be able to show that impassibility means apathy or absence of concern for creation. Not only can we manifestly not do this, it is abundantly clear from the beginning that if impassibility were understood in this way it would amount to a grave moral error.

Indeed, Augustine suggests as much when he rhetorically asks, referring to the Greek term for impassibility: 'if *apatheia* is the name of the state in which the mind cannot be touched by any emotion whatsoever, who would not judge this insensitivity to be the worst of all moral defects?'[33] While the Greek term for impassibility, *apatheia*, may be superficially more susceptible to the kind of critique the advocates of a suffering God wish to make, if we take the time to understand what is and is not being said about God we will realize that in no way does *apatheia* imply apathy. Quite the contrary, David Bentley Hart suggests that *apatheia* should be 'defined as infinitely active love; it does not require our sin and death to show us "mercy": God loved us when we were not, and by this very "mercy" called us into being. And this is the ground of all our hope.'[34]

The critique that launches the notion of a suffering God in the first place thereby rests on a highly dubious caricature of the tradition of Christian thinking about the relationship between God and evil. More serious still, however, are problems inherent in the notion of a suffering God itself, only one of which we will elaborate on here:

> As many of the fathers would have argued, a God who can by nature experience finite affects and so be determined by them is a God whose identity is established through a commerce with evil; if the nature of God's love can be in any sense positively shaped by sin, suffering, and death, then sin, suffering, and death will always be in some sense features of who he is. Among other things, this means that evil must enjoy a certain independent authenticity, a reality with which God must come to grips, and God's love must be inherently deficient.

Goodness then requires evil to be good; love must be goaded into being by pain.[35]

So while the proponents of a suffering God want to affirm, above all, the compassion of God with respect to human suffering, they open themselves up to the possibility of implicating God in the very existence of the evils suffered by humanity because they are in some sense constitutive of God's own identity. If God needs to suffer in order to love, as Moltmann argues, then suffering and violence become a necessary part of Christ's saving work and evil is something that must be defeated for God to be God. It is difficult to imagine this suffering God as anything more than one who has the same kinds of concerns that we do, as yet another inhabitant of our moral world.

Redeeming Sorrows

It is a peculiarly modern argument that makes us think that our suffering necessitates such a radical re-conception of God. Unfortunately, the twentieth century has no monopoly on suffering as earlier generations witnessed horrible events of their own yet they did not think this called into question the doctrine of God. One of the most devastating pandemics in recorded human history is the plague commonly known as the Black Death, which swept through Europe and was at its peak between 1348 and 1350. People died horribly and suddenly in great numbers, with estimates claiming that somewhere between 30 and 60 per cent of the population was wiped out. The plague was so contagious that witnesses describe how anyone who so much as touched a sick or dying person caught the disease and died themselves, which necessitated mass burial sites, some of which have been discovered only recently. The effects were devastating and were exacerbated by further unpredictable outbreaks and the social and political unrest that then ensued. In the midst of this situation of death, turmoil and socio-political upheaval, Julian of Norwich (c.1342–1416) offers a profound meditation on the nature of divine love that makes no pretensions about altering the doctrine of God in the light of the calamities of her day. On the contrary, the conclusion that Julian draws from her meditations on a series of 'showings' that centred around a vision of the bloody face of Christ is that suffering is transient. Though we know very little of the details of Julian's life, her reflections on the mystery of human suffering stand firmly in the Augustinian tradition that understands evil as a lack of goodness.[36] For Julian it is precisely because evil has no substance that we can look forward to a day when all sorrows will be redeemed:

> Suddenly you will be taken out of all your pain, all your sickness, all your unrest and all your woe. And you will come up above, and you will have me for your reward, and you will be filled full of joy and bliss, and you will never again have any kind of pain, any kind of sickness, any kind of displeasure, no lack of will, but always joy and bliss without end.[37]

Julian's reflections could well be a meditation on the passages from Revelation with which we began this chapter (Rev. 21:3–5). Her understanding of evil as a lack of goodness is the ground of all our hope and is what prompts her to affirm, with the seer of Revelation, that 'all shall be well, and all manner of things shall be well'.[38] All of this is to say, then, that to seek to understand God and the mystery of human suffering requires us to think more deeply than we have with the Christian tradition because there is much more at stake in the treatment of impassibility than it would seem from the dismissals of it by many contemporary theologians.

9.

God in History

What surprises me, says God, is hope.
And I can't get over it.
This little hope who seems like nothing at all.
This little girl hope.
Immortal.

It's she, the little one, who carries them all.
Because Faith sees only what is.
But she, she sees what will be.
Charity loves only what is.
But she, she loves what will be.

– Charles Péguy (1873–1914)[1]

An Audacious Hope

An examination of the God of history or of God in history is, in Christian terms, a question of eschatology, that is to say, a question about the final outcome and transformation of history. One of the deepest divisions in contemporary thinking on this question is between those who think a dramatic story can indeed be told about reality as a whole and those who do not. For some time now the incessant clang of 'postmodernism' has cast suspicion on the very possibility of 'classical notions of truth, reason, identity, universal progress, grand narratives and ultimate grounds of explanation'.[2] The very possibility of the claims of much of the postmodern critique itself can be understood as an outworking of mistakes in Christian theology, although this is an argument for another time.

In contrast to the 'postmodern' narratives of suspicion with which we are confronted today, the Christian tradition is deeply invested in what can only seem like an audacious and insane hope of a kingdom of peace and justice that encompasses all of creation, a vision of reconciliation in which suffering and death are wiped away (Rev. 21:3–5). Perhaps even more incredibly, the Christian tradition makes the claim that the kingdom of God is the completion of all things and has already been made visible within history in the person and work of Jesus Christ. In the light of the cross and resurrection, the Christian tradition claims that God has reversed all the 'necessary' truths of history, all our own narratives of power and domination, and declared the story of his infinite peace, which is the ground of all our hope. This grandest of all stories occurs within a particular history: in creation and covenant, in the election of Israel, in the life of Jesus and in the body of Christ, the church. In the face of false tales of original violence, suffering and death, the Christian tradition must direct its attention incessantly back toward God whose sovereignty relativizes and reorients all our own claims to power and self-sufficiency. If we do so, we too might be able to glimpse something of the Christian character of hope, of a hope beyond mere optimism that enabled Julian of Norwich to proclaim with confidence that 'all shall be well'.

The Beginnings of Eschatology in Scripture

The biblical witness contains many different accounts of the end of history that are not easily harmonized. Despite the many interesting specificities and undulating terrain that makes up the biblical account we can nevertheless postulate that these different scenarios are all part of one single occurrence, one event that is the event of God's own actuality, that is, the event of the triune life itself. Language is here again stretched to its breaking point because nothing else comes after the event in question. Nevertheless, we must note from the outset that eschatology is from beginning to end a political discourse. In the promise to Abraham and the writings of the prophets, the eschaton is the fulfilment of Israel's political structures. Likewise, in the gospel accounts it is a 'kingdom', a fact that even the Roman authorities perceived. Because eschatology examines the God who acts in history, it is therefore necessarily caught up with issues of authority, power and judgement and begins, as Oliver O'Donovan reminds us, with the statement: 'Yhwh reigns.'[3]

If we turn more specifically to the biblical witness we are immediately confronted by its political character. The initial call of Abram that founded Israel was not to create a new cult or pattern of ritual piety but rather to lead a migration (Gen. 12:1). The summons of God comes with a promise that not only will Israel be established as a great nation but also that their greatness will consist in being a blessing to other nations (Gen. 12:2–3). So God's creation of the covenant with Israel occurs as a political act. Reflecting on this aspect, Walter Brueggemann suggests that the covenant represents 'a radical and systemic alternative to the politics of autonomy, the economics of exploitation and the theology of self-indulgence'.[4]

How this nation, brought into existence by the covenant with God, is to be governed is a matter of intense dispute that raged throughout Israel's history although it was clear all along that this nation contained within it a universal promise that it should be the 'priestly kingdom' for the other nations (Exod. 19:5–6). As we have noted in previous chapters, a monarchy was eventually established so that Israel could be 'like other nations' although this too had its peculiarities. Even David had to be legitimated by himself being a prophet (2 Sam. 23:1–2). Furthermore, Israel's kings were always subject to rebuke by the prophets who claimed to overrule them with the word of God. So even though Israel's monarchy became more established, with a capital city and more common economic and military trappings, it was always subject to the demands of the covenant and in the wake of its long undoing its political hopes were explicitly focused on a vision of eschatological peace: 'He shall judge between many peoples, and shall arbitrate between strong nations far away; they shall beat their swords into ploughshares, and their spears into pruning hooks; nation shall not lift up sword against nation, neither shall they learn war any more' (Mic. 4:1–3). Simply put, the age to come is envisioned as a universal polity of peace.

If the story ended there we might be forgiven for imagining that whatever sought-after peace was being described in Scripture was undoubtedly a very long way off. However, it was not long before Jesus was proclaiming that 'the time is fulfilled, and the kingdom of God has come near' (Mark 1:15). With this annunciation, the possibility of this polity of peace became a present reality. That the age to come had drawn near had profound effects for the powers and institutions that claimed for themselves a necessary or self-sufficient status. Indeed, the good news of the gospel is graphically displayed in the reversal of self-aggrandizing orderings of power: rulers are brought down from their thrones, the lowly are lifted up, the hungry are filled and the rich are sent away empty (Luke 1:46–55). From the perspective of Pilate, Jesus' proclamation of the kingdom must have seemed little more than ridiculous nonsense. Was he oblivious to the lowliness of his state and to the magnitude of the powers into whose hands he had been delivered? However, by the light of the resurrection, in and through the visibility of the empty tomb, we are enabled to see that the assumed sovereignty of the powers that enslave us is in fact subordinate to God (Col. 1:15–17).[5]

The Apocalyptic Politics of Jesus

If we want to get a clearer sense of what this subversive kingdom looks like we can do no better that to turn to the concluding chapter of *The Politics of Jesus*. Here Yoder seeks to make historical sense of the meaning of the apocalyptic vision of the seer of Patmos in the book of Revelation. The connections Yoder makes between cross and resurrection, power and non-violence, and the meaning and direction of history are indispensable for our purposes.

For Yoder, the apocalyptic politics of Jesus are linked from beginning to end with the question of violence and what form Jesus' kingship will take. He notes that in the modern age we are particularly obsessed with the meaning and direction of history, which is by no means simply an idle philosophical concern but is itself a corollary of the biblical claim that God is active in history. In the face of this and through a close reading of Scripture Yoder develops what he calls a 'biblical philosophy of history' that is 'nothing more than a logical unfolding of the meaning of the work of Jesus Christ himself, whose choice of suffering servanthood rather than violent lordship, of love to the point of death rather than righteousness backed by power, was itself the fundamental direction of his life'.[6] While the first eleven chapters of *The Politics of Jesus* are devoted to a close reading of the Gospel of Luke and of the apostolic tradition primarily in the letters of St Paul, what is most important here for our present purposes is Yoder's reading of the series of visions and hymns as recounted by John of Patmos:

> Then I saw in the right hand of the one seated on the throne a scroll written on the inside and on the back, sealed with seven seals; and I saw a mighty angel proclaiming with a loud voice, 'Who is worthy to open the scroll and break its seals?' And no one in heaven or on earth or under the earth was able to open the scroll or to look into it. And I began to weep bitterly . . . Then I looked, and I heard the voice of many angels . . . singing with full voice,
>
>> Worthy is the Lamb that was
>>> slaughtered
>> to receive power and wealth and
>>> wisdom and might
>> and honour and glory and blessing! (Rev. 5:1–12)

The question of the meaningfulness of history is here laid bare and that the slaughtered Lamb alone is able to open the scroll means that suffering and not coercive power determines the meaning of history. The scandal here is not a simple refusal of power, a perverse glorification of weakness or even a choice between obedience and effectiveness but rather that Christian discipleship aims to cleave so closely to the person and work of Jesus Christ that it is willing to accept defeat rather than complicity with evil. It is this kind of cruciform discipleship that is aligned with the ultimate triumph of the Lamb. As Yoder puts it, 'Jesus chose the cross as an alternative social strategy of strength, not weakness.'[7]

Key to this understanding of the apocalyptic politics of Jesus is the biblical virtue of patience that is perhaps the most crucial in a world where we seem to be incessantly looking for ways that we can move history in whatever direction we think best. In this sense, Yoder's biblical philosophy of history is in deep sympathy with Hans Urs von Balthasar's theology of history, which, likewise, highlights the centrality of patience in the New Testament. In a passage that could just as easily have been penned by Yoder, Balthasar claims that patience:

> becomes the basic constituent of Christianity, more central even than humility: the power to wait, to persevere, to hold out, to endure to the end, not to transcend one's own limitations, not to force issues by playing the hero or the titan, but to practice the virtue that lies beyond heroism, the meekness of the lamb, which is *led*.[8]

What both Balthasar and Yoder are at pains to emphasize is that to practise the virtue of patience is no simple refusal of action but is itself the outworking of a different kind of power, a meekness beyond heroism. Yoder repeatedly returns to this dynamic throughout his work and, with unintentional echoes of Balthasar, highlights the 'almighty meekness of the reigning Lord' by arguing that:

> when the Christian whom God has disarmed lays aside carnal weapons it is not, in the last analysis, because those weapons are too strong, but because they are too weak. He directs his life toward the day when all creation will praise not kings and chancellors but the Lamb that was slain as worthy to receive blessing and honor and glory *and power* (Rev. 5:12–13).[9]

Echoing this sentiment again much later, Yoder readily concedes that non-violence may, in some cases, refer to nothing more than a principled or pragmatic rejection of violence but argues instead for a form of non-violent action that renounces violence 'in order that other kinds of power (truth, consent, conscience) may work'.[10]

Thus it should be abundantly clear that to understand Yoder as promulgating a politics of despair that simply renounces effectiveness is a gross misreading. His frankness in admitting that 'we cannot sight down the barrel of suffering love to see how it will hit its target'[11] highlights not some form of tragic resignation to the bloody theatre of history but rather that, if hope is to be particularly Christian, it must be conformed to what it proclaims. Put negatively, the cross is not a recipe for resurrection. In this way, we can see that the exercise of patience has the effect of breaking through the mechanistic logic that dominates the workings of the interpretive grids through which we attempt to steer history in the right direction. However, the divine patience that Yoder is at pains to emphasize is not simply a *breaking through* but also a *breaking forth*. That is, alongside its power to 'relativize both the gloomy and the confident determinisms to which we have been captive'[12] is the production of a context for creativity that a commitment to non-violence enables. The 'power' of 'non-violence', then, is necessarily bound up with the apocalyptic politics of Jesus and not simply an optional addition.

Put differently, what Yoder calls the 'pacifism of the messianic community' is subordinate to and arises out of a vision that puts its hope in the theological claim that Jesus Christ is Lord. For this reason, Yoder describes non-violence as a 'distinctive spirituality . . . [that] presupposes and fosters a distinctive way of seeing oneself and one's neighbor under God'.[13] In what is perhaps his most complete description of this particular mode of vision Yoder argues that it is best understood as doxology, which is, as he writes, 'a way of seeing; a grasp of which end is up, which way is forward'.[14] In a particularly revealing passage Yoder helpfully connects his mode of vision with the creative *breaking forth* of hope by arguing that 'to see history doxologically means that the criterion most apt for validating a disposition, a decision, an action, is not the predictable success before it but the resurrection behind it, not manipulation but praise. Hope is not a reflex rebounding from defeat but a reflection of theophany.'[15]

People of Hope

Where does this leave us, then? How is it possible to participate in this audacious hope today? Holocaust survivor Elie Wiesel suggests that we must try to find a language that promotes solidarity, especially with the outcast, the oppressed and the victimized:

> Let us tell tales. Let us tell tales – all the rest can wait, all the rest can wait. Let us tell tales – that is our primary obligation. Tales of children

so wise and so old. Tales of old men mute with fear. Tales of victims welcoming death as an old acquaintance. Tales that bring men close to the abyss and beyond – and others that lift him up to heaven and beyond. Tales of immense flames reaching out the sky, tales of night consuming life and hope and eternity. Let us tell tales so as to remember how vulnerable man is when faced with overwhelming evil. Let us tell tales so as not to allow the executioner to have the last word.[16]

Of course, not all the tales we tell will be ones that reflect the glory of God. Moreover, we shall also have to pay close attention to how we tell our tales because the potential for misremembering is ever-present. With those caveats in mind, we would like to suggest that we can see one such creative interweaving of doxology, non-violence and patience in the distinctive spirituality embodied in the theological life of Dorothy Day (1897–1980).

Born into a middle-class family in Brooklyn, New York, Day spent much of her youth struggling through the relationship between religion and her commitment to social activism. In her autobiography she writes: 'I felt my faith had nothing to do with that of Christians around me.'[17] Day longed for a reconciliation of body and spirit, belief and experience, justice and charity. Her reception into the Roman Catholic Church in 1927 was itself part of the outworking of her struggle to integrate faith and justice. She observes that 'it was the great mass of the poor, the workers, who were the Catholics in this country, and this fact drew me to the Church'.[18] Day did not rest content in the bosom of the church, however, because she found 'plenty of charity, but too little justice'.[19] Her life-long struggle with this discovery led her to embody the presence of Christ in humanity in ways that disturbed the comfortable status quo. Together with Peter Maurin, Day founded what became known as the Catholic Worker Movement, which is perhaps best known for its publication *The Catholic Worker*, which was first published on 1 May 1933, and for its houses of hospitality that opened across the country in service to the homeless. It would not be going too far to say that Day's life is one example of the outworking of what it means to believe in the presence of Christ in the world and in the communion of his body that we call the church.

The theopolitical vision articulated by Day is difficult to encapsulate as it exceeds notions of anarchism, Christian communitarianism, and non-violent localism while including aspects of each of these. One entry point, however, is particularly apt for our purposes. In her reflection on the efficacy of the Catholic Worker Movement, Day helpfully articulates the workings of her vision:

> How little we have attempted, let alone accomplished. The consolation is this – and this is our faith too: By our sufferings and our failures, by our acceptance of the Cross, by our struggle to grow in faith, hope, and charity, we unleash forces that help to overcome evil in the world.[20]

For Day, the embodiment of this hope in the world was necessarily bound up with active non-violence, which in her case sometimes led to acts of civil disobedience. She was willing to go to jail for some of these acts and did spend time in prison; however, she was not committed to civil disobedience for its own sake. On the contrary, Day's vision is rooted in Jesus' proclamation that the kingdom of God that brings good news for the poor has been fulfilled (Luke 4:18–21). What this means, as Paul reminds us, is that we cannot be conformed to the ways of the world (Rom. 12:2).

One of the very practical ways that Day and the Catholic Worker Movement embodied this was through tax resistance. However, instead of simply refusing to pay the percentage of taxes that were used by the state to support the military industrial complex, Day and the Catholic Worker Movement refused to pay in a more radical way: by choosing to live below the poverty line where no taxes have to be paid. This has the effect of grounding the practice of non-violence in everyday living and vividly exposes the connection between military spending and social inequality. Moreover, it is a form of love because it actively chooses to refuse to support the killing of enemies of the state. This practice has led some to rightly observe that 'Worker houses have themselves been a daily, living laboratory of experiments in nonviolence'.[21] These experiments open a space for creativity and are examples of the *breaking forth* of the new creation here and now. Thus we may conclude, with Yoder, that Day's life itself embodies something of the meekness of the Lamb because she rightly saw that suffering love and servanthood are 'more adequate definitions of doing the will of God than are tactical projections about how to maximize the likelihood of bringing about certain desirable states of the total social system'.[22]

Practices of Hope

It must immediately be said that by pointing to a specific individual we do not wish to make the claim that Christianity needs heroes to flourish. On the contrary, we are convinced that to tell the Christian story in an epic tone is to distort it out of all recognition. This is one of the reasons that the theological life of Dorothy Day is so apt for our purposes: her work points away from itself to the infinite life of the Triune God in which it imperfectly participates. In a sense, Day's life was not her own, caught up as it was in the body of Christ in service to the wretched of the earth. Indeed, Day describes the Catholic Worker Movement as a re-membering of the body of Christ:

> This teaching, the doctrine of the Mystical Body of Christ, involves today the issue of unions (where men call each other brothers); it involves the racial question; it involves cooperatives; credit unions; it involves Houses of Hospitality and farming communities. It is with all these means that we can live as though we believed indeed that we are all members of one another, knowing that when 'the health of one member suffers, the health of the whole body is lowered' [1 Cor. 12:26].[23]

Thus our task, is a communal one or more accurately an ecclesial one. What Day realized is that living in solidarity with the poor is the way of embodying God's love because it enacts the kingdom that Jesus proclaimed had already begun here on earth.

How, then, is the body of Christ to go about its business of making decisions, distributing power, assigning roles? In short, how is the body of Christ, the church, supposed to function and organize itself? Yoder suggests that 'the will of God for human socialness as a whole is prefigured by the shape to which the body of Christ is called . . . The people of God is called to be today what the world is called to be ultimately.'[24] He goes on to suggest that we can discern five practices that the church is called to embody: binding and loosing, breaking bread, baptism, gift discernment and open meeting. For reasons of space we shall focus only on one of these practices, namely the Eucharist. Every celebration of the Lord's Supper begins as Jesus commands his followers: 'Do this in remembrance of me' (Luke 22:19). Yoder rightly emphasizes that what we now think of as a 'ceremony' that occurs on Sunday mornings, or sadly only a select few Sundays every year in some churches, is actually a profound economic act of sharing in which there is no longer anyone in need (Acts 4:34).[25] While we do not wish to demur from this insight we are convinced that the meaning of the Eucharist is not confined to economic sharing. Indeed, the celebration of the Eucharist is not simply a recollection of a past event with significant economic implications but a re-membering of the body of Christ itself. One of the most insightful theologians of our day puts it like this:

> The point of saying the Eucharist makes the church is that the body of Christ is not a perduring institution which moves linearly through time, but must be constantly received anew in the Eucharistic action. Christ is not the possession of the church, but is always being given to the church, which in turn gives Christ away.[26]

In fact, this insight that the Eucharist makes the church can deepen and extend Yoder's emphasis on the economic aspect of the Lord's Supper. If the Eucharist makes the church, the body of Christ, then it is also the site par excellence of resistance to our contemporary culture of consumerism. As Jesus says, 'those who eat my flesh and drink my blood abide in me, *and I in them*' (John 6:56). Here the act of consumption is turned inside out because instead of simply consuming the body of Christ, we are consumed by it.[27] So while it is instructive for us to see that the Lord's Supper must be one in which all are fed, in our day it is just as crucial to see that in the eucharistic feast we ourselves are incorporated into Christ. It is this incorporation into Christ's body that enables us to participate in the infinite life of the Triune God, who makes our lives possible.

Conclusion

> I am the Alpha and the Omega,
> the first and the last,
> the beginning and the end.
>
> – Revelation 22:13

It simply is not possible to conclude what is going on in this book. The best we can do is gather up the argument and then begin again. Talk about God is like that.

We have written about God, or at least that has been our intention, the goal for which we have striven. As far as we are concerned there is nothing more important for us or anyone else to think, speak and write about. We are aware that important books are written about mission, worship, the church, discipleship and much else but at the heart of these, when properly addressed, is God. What is the first commandment? It is to love God with all our heart, soul, strength and mind and our neighbour as ourselves (Mark 12:29–30). God alone is the heart of the matter. We wish the deep questions about God, the theological questions, might be taken with more confidence and urgency by everyone, not least the church.

We are aware that Christians who live in Europe and North America share the territory with an increasing number of people who are simply indifferent to talk about God. They don't bother for various reasons, one of which is that they see no point, no usefulness in the language. Hence to say something is theological has come to mean it is largely irrelevant. In the much-quoted assertion of the French mathematician Pierre-Simon Laplace (1749–1824), people have come to believe that there is no need for a God hypothesis. So they dismiss talk of God.

Perhaps because we have not listened as carefully to Scripture as we should, and have not paid attention to the painstaking tradition of speech about God in the story of the church we have fallen into the temptation of shaping God after our presumed acceptable ideas of God, acceptable to us that is. So the almighty warrior, the supporter of armies, one who blesses nuclear submarines, a kind of superman who can jump over high buildings and do many other things we cannot do comes to be praised and served. Then attempts are made to market these pictures, for their therapeutic value, their sustaining of a community of our kind of people, to show how 'relevant' God is to us, how tolerant and welcoming God is. Such theologies become competitive, as soundness or effectiveness in gaining numbers is made the criterion of truth. God looks remarkably of our making, the supporter of our denomination, or national identity: 'Our God reigns!' Behind this may well be the earnest desire to communicate news by promoting our own religious group, but is this the good news of God?

Thinking and speaking about God is difficult, and not just intellectually hard. The Bible bears its own witness to the temptation to make God in our image, to forget that we are creatures. When the nations are in uproar, making war and fighting their corner, God does not come cheering on one side against another. Instead we hear the command: 'Be still, stop your fighting, and know that I am God' (see Ps. 46:10). There are warnings about easy verbiage concerning God. From the Wisdom tradition comes the advice, 'Never be rash with your mouth, nor let your heart be quick to utter a word before God, for God is in heaven, and you upon earth; therefore let your words be few' (Eccl. 5:2). On our own, we simply cannot speak about God before whom the proper response is silence.

We have argued, with the Bible and the tradition of Christian speaking, that God is not part of the world we know and share. God is the creator of this universe of universes, of all that is. God is not in a class of beings called divine, like the gods of our making. God is not some holy thing, a possible object of our knowing. God is beyond, transcendent, and yet is the One in whom we live and move and have our being (Acts 17:28). The startling claim, the good news Christians have to tell is that we can speak of God, not because we are clever, or especially devout, but because God has spoken. God has spoken in the story of Israel, in his dealings with the world but primarily, crucially, in the person and work of Jesus Christ. This particular focus may sound troubling to those who look for inclusive pluralism to be sign of the faith by which we live but it is the belief to which the Scriptures and the church bear witness.

So what shall we say to our contemporaries, young or old, who know that in our plural society there are a number of religions on offer? They ask, why should we follow Jesus? Why not the way of Islam taught by Mohammed, or the peaceful reflections of the Buddha? Why do we need anyone to teach us? Can't we simply take responsibility for ourselves and work it out? Why Jesus? We could make an argument that it would be a much better world if people lived the way of Jesus. While we would not disagree with this argument we nevertheless find it deeply wanting. We would want to assert that we follow Jesus and proclaim him as good news because he is the unique revelation of God, God the Son, the Word Incarnate. The otherwise unknowable God, radically beyond us and all our words, has spoken to us. All those arguments about God in Trinity are attempts to speak this fundamental truth.

It has also been our argument that language is not vague speculation about the unknowable God but has massive implications for our living, our calling as the church, our politics and practices now. There are few subjects as practical as theology, for the meaning of words is inseparable from living. It is no accident that we have found ourselves speaking of peace and peacemaking in this broken tribal world as we have recalled the language of Trinity. We have done so, not out of any wishfulness but because the language of God leads us in the ways of reconciliation and peace. We need to hear the call of this peacemaking, peace-giving God. Other gods of nationalism, militarism, consumerism, make quite enough noise of their own. It is the Triune God who speaks the word of liberation, leading us in the way of peace.

All this is to recall the arguments we have tried to spell out. We have deliberately drawn on the Bible as our primary source. But we have also tried to listen to the Christian tradition that, like us, struggles us to speak truthfully and honestly of God. We have gone outside our own denominational homes for this resource and done so unashamedly, in gratitude for the tradition we neglect at our peril. So much hangs on how we speak of God. Following the false gods leads back to slavery, to violence and fear. Casualness about God leads to human-centred religiosity. We have seen in the last century how wrong thoughts of God, irreverence and easy assumptions about God and ourselves can lead to frightening disasters. Indeed, religion of our making is a sign of our lack of trust in the true God. Dietrich Bonhoeffer saw this. In June 1932 he preached against the government's misuse of God's name:

> Our disobedience is not that we are so irreligious, but that we are very glad to be religious . . . very relieved when some government proclaims the Christian worldview . . . so that the more pious we are, the less we let ourselves be told that God is dangerous, that God will not be mocked.[1]

Does it ever cross the minds of contemporary worshippers that 'It is a fearful thing to fall into the hands of the living God' (Heb. 10:31)?

There is an urgent need especially for Christians to learn to speak again of God. There is no subject as crucial as God, our creator and saviour, the one known in Jesus by the power of the Spirit. God is our hope in a world often capable of sinking into deep darkness.

But for all our speaking there remains a necessary caution. For all God's self-revelation, for all our hearing of the good news from the witnesses, our speech calls for modesty. Our vision of God is not totally clear but it will not always be like this (1 Cor. 13:12). We must not teach our dogmas too dogmatically. We are speaking of God who is beyond our theological constructions, even those grounded in revelation. Our words about God as Father, Son, Spirit, Trinity are all words of truth but not the whole truth. It is given to us to name but not to exhaustively describe the first and the last and the Living One.

Which all leads us to worship, to wondering, to paying attention, to prayer, to a life of response to God who made us. We are called together to be the body of Christ in and for the world. We name God as Trinity. We feed the hungry. We listen to the Bible. We visit those in prison. We sing hymns and offer prayers. We come to the table and receive more than bread and wine. We bind up that which is broken. By the work of the gracious Spirit we are led deeper into the life of God, which is to say, deeper into communion with each other. We comfort the sorrowful. We are found by grace. Our thankfulness abounds. Our hope is renewed. Our debts are forgiven. We forgive our debtors. Heaven and earth meet, for God is among us. We lose ourselves in wonder, love and praise, in the life of God:

> Now the Lord is the Spirit, and where the Spirit of the Lord is, there is freedom. And all of us, with unveiled faces, seeing the glory of the Lord as though reflected in a mirror, are being transformed into the same image from one degree of glory to another; for this comes from the Lord, the Spirit (2 Cor. 3:17–18).

Endnotes

Introduction

[1] Voltaire, *The Works of Voltaire: The Lisbon Earthquake and Other Poems*, ed. by Tobias George Smollett, et al. Vol. XXVI (Akron: The Werner Company), 1901, p. 16.
[2] Charles Davy, 'The Earthquake at Lisbon, 1755', in *Modern History Sourcebook*, http://www.fordham.edu/halsall/mod/1755lisbonquake.asp (accessed 9 Oct. 2013).
[3] John Howard Yoder, *The Original Revolution: Essays on Christian Pacifism* (Scottdale: Herald Press, 2003), pp. 65-6.
[4] Esther Addley, 'Atheist Sunday Assembly branches out in first wave of expansion', *The Guardian* (2013).
http://www.theguardian.com/world/2013/sep/14/atheist-sunday-assembly-branches-out (accessed 14 Sept. 2013).
[5] See, for example, Alain de Botton, *Religion for Atheists: A Non-Believer's Guide to the Uses of Religion* (London: Penguin, 2013).
[6] See Tim Newell, *Forgiving Justice: A Quaker Vision for Criminal Justice* (London, Quaker Home Service, 2000). A very helpful introduction to the issues can be found in Howard Zehr, *The Little Book of Restorative Justice* (Intercourse: Good Books, 2002).
[7] A. James Reimer, 'Mennonites, Christ, and Culture: The Yoder Legacy', in *Mennonites and Classical Theology: Dogmatic Foundations for Christian Ethics* (Kitchener: Pandora Press, 2001), p. 295.
[8] Oliver O'Donovan, *The Desire of the Nations: Rediscovering the Roots of* Political Theology (New York: Cambridge University Press, 1999), p. ix.
[9] See G.K. Chesterton, *St. Thomas Aquinas* (San Rafael: Angelico Press, 2011), pp. 3–24.

10. See Hans Urs von Balthasar, *Truth is Symphonic: Aspects of Christian Pluralism*, trans. Graham Harrison (San Francisco: Ignatius Press, 1987).

1. God in Scripture

1. All biblical references are taken from the New Revised Standard Version unless otherwise stated.
2. We have in mind here, for example, the writings of Richard Dawkins, Daniel Dennett, Sam Harris and Christopher Hitchens, sometimes called the 'new atheists'.
3. John Howard Yoder, *The Original Revolution: Essays on Christian Pacifism* (Scottdale: Herald Press, 2003), p. 65.
4. See Walter Brueggemann, 'The Prophet as Destabilizing Presence', in *The Pastor as Prophet* ed. Earl E. Shelp and Ronald H. Sunderland (New York: Pilgrim Press, 1985), pp. 49ff.
5. See 'The Fate of Ideas: Moses', in Marilynne Robinson, *When I was a Child I Read Books* (New York: Picador, 2012), pp. 95–124.
6. We have in mind here, for example, God's calling of Cyrus the Persian who is called the anointed of God in Isa. 45:1.
7. Herbert McCabe, OP, *God Still Matters* (London: Continuum, 2002), p. 3.

2. God with Us

1. The phrase 'kingdom of heaven' is from Matthew who shows a Jewish respect fort the name of God. The phrase means the kingdom of God.
2. Messiah is a Hebrew word meaning Anointed One. In Greek the word is Christ. There is continuing debate as to how deep was the conviction in Israel about the coming Christ, who he would be and what would be his role in God's saving work.
3. This is the case with the Synoptic Gospels. John tells of several visits Jesus paid to the city.
4. See Peter J. Leithart, *Defending Constantine: The Twilight of an Empire and the Dawn of Christendom* (Downers Grove: InterVarsity Press, 2010), especially pp. 223–4. Leithart also argues that while the liberation of slaves was nothing new, Constantine's innovation was to make the

liberation of slaves within the church an act of piety that was pleasing to God.
5. We wish to go even further here to note that some of the reforms instituted by Constantine are consonant with a life of discipleship, which, as Yoder reminds us, may include 'opening the court system to conflict resolution procedures', in John Howard Yoder, *Body Politics: Five Practices for the Christian Church Before the Watching World* (Scottdale: Herald Press, 2001), p. 27. Yoder's wider comments here also bear a striking resemblance to Gregory's Fourth Sermon on Ecclesiastes.
6. Gregory of Nyssa, 'Homilies on Ecclesiastes,' in *Gregory of Nyssa: Homilies on Ecclesiastes*, ed. Stuart George Hall (Berlin: W. de Gruyter, 1993), p. 74.
7. Thomas Helwys, *A Short Declaration of the Mystery of Iniquity* (London: Baptist Historical Society, 1935).
8. For a full examination of Helwys' argument see Brian Haymes, 'Thomas Helwys' The Mystery of Iniquity: Is it Still Relevant in the Twenty-First Century?,' in *Exploring Baptist Origins*, ed. Anthony R. Cross and Nicholas J. Wood (Oxford: Regent's Park College, 2010), 61-77.
9. As cited in Andrew Bradstock and Christopher Rowland, ed. *Radical Christian Writings* (Oxford: Blackwell, 2002), pp. 201–2.

3. God the Spirit

1. Some teachers think this is why John's account of the cleansing of the temple comes early in the story of Jesus (John 2:13–22).
2. Samuel Wells, *Improvisation: The Drama of Christian Ethics* (Grand Rapids: Brazos Press, 2004).
3. John Driver, *Radical Faith: An Alternative History of the Christian Church* (Kitchener: Pandora Press, 1999).
4. Walter H. Burgess, *The Pastor of the Pilgrims: A Biography of John Robinson* (New York: Harcourt, Brace & Howe, 1920), pp. 239–40.
5. For example, the King James Version of 1611.
6. John Howard Yoder, *Revolutionary Christianity: The 1966 South American Lectures*, ed. Paul Martens, et al. (Eugene: Cascade, 2011), p. 140.

4. The Triune God

[1] NKJV, translation slightly modified. This text is often referred to as the 'Johannine Comma' and does not appear in most early Greek manuscripts.

[2] Ludwig Wittgenstein, *Culture and Value*, trans. Peter Winch (Oxford: Blackwell, rev. edn, 1998), p. 97e.

[3] John Howard Yoder, *Preface to Theology: Christology and Theological Method* (Grand Rapids: Brazos, 2002), p. 204. Perhaps more strongly, Yoder argues that 'it seems that the only claim of the Nicene Creed is to have provided the best answer to an intellectual problem' (p. 205).

[4] Yoder, *Preface to Theology*, pp. 204–5.

[5] This view is succinctly summed up in Yoder's argument that 'what the churches accepted in the Constantinian shift is what Jesus had rejected, seizing godlikeness, moving in hoc signo from Golgotha to the battlefield' in John Howard Yoder, 'The Constantinian Sources of Western Social Ethics', in *The Priestly Kingdom: Social Ethics as Gospel* (Notre Dame: University of Notre Dame Press, 1984), p. 145.

[6] John Howard Yoder, *The Politics of Jesus: Vicit Agnus Noster* (Grand Rapids: Eerdmans, 2nd edn, 1998), pp. 102–4.

[7] See Aristotle, 'Physics', in *The Complete Works of Aristotle*, ed. Jonathan Barnes (Princeton: Princeton University Press, 1984), p. 315.

[8] Augustine, *On Christian Teaching*, trans. R.P.H. Green (New York: Oxford University Press, 1997, pp. 6–7.

[9] John Henry Newman, *An Essay on the Development of Christian Doctrine* (Notre Dame: University of Notre Dame Press, 6th edn, 1989), p. 40.

[10] For a brilliant explication of this unity in difference see especially G.K. Chesterton, *St. Thomas Aquinas* (San Rafael: Angelico Press, 2011), pp. 3–24.

[11] Augustine, *On Christian Teaching*, p. 117.

[12] See Samuel Wells, *Improvisation: The Drama of Christian Ethics* (Grand Rapids: Brazos Press, 2004), especially pp. 59-70.

[13] Augustine, *The Trinity*, trans. Edmund Hill, OP (New York: New City Press, 2nd edn, 2012), p. 68 [Book I.1.5].

[14] A brief sketch is the best we can hope to accomplish as the history is complex and contested to this day. For a reliable and nuanced account, which we have broadly followed, see Lewis Ayres, *Nicaea and Its Legacy: An Approach to Fourth-Century Trinitarian Theology* (New York: Oxford University Press, 2004).

15. As cited in Ayres, *Nicaea and Its Legacy*, p. 19.
16. See Daniel H. Williams, 'Constantine and the "Fall" of the Church', in *Christian Origins: Theology, Rhetoric and Community*, ed. Lewis Ayres and Gareth Jones (New York: Routledge, 1998), pp. 117–36.
17. See Ayres, *Nicaea and Its Legacy*, pp. 85–104.
18. For a wonderful reflection on this see the theological postscript in Rowan Williams, *Arius: Heresy and Tradition* (London: SCM, 2nd edn, 2001), pp. 233–45.
19. Basil of Caesarea, 'Letter CLIX', in *Nicene and Post-Nicene Fathers*, ed. Philip Schaff and Henry Wace (Edinburgh: T&T Clark, 1994), p. 613.
20. Basil of Caesarea, 'Letter XXXVIII', in *Nicene and Post-Nicene Fathers*, ed. Philip Schaff and Henry Wace (Edinburgh: T&T Clark, 1994), pp. 430–31.
21. Gregory of Nyssa, 'On the Holy Spirit', in *Nicene and Post-Nicene Fathers*, ed. Philip Schaff and Henry Wace (Edinburgh: T&T Clark, 1994), p. 601.
22. Augustine, *The Trinity*, p. 197 [Book V.2.11].
23. Augustine, *The Trinity*, p. 285 [Book IX.3.18].
24. Augustine, *The Trinity*, p. 210 [Book VI.5.7].
25. Immanuel Kant, 'The Conflict of the Faculties', in *Religion and Rational Theology*, ed. Allen W. Wood and George di Giovanni (Cambridge: Cambridge University Press, 2001), p. 264.
26. See Friedrich Schleiermacher, *The Christian Faith*, trans. H.R. Mackintosh and J.S. Stewart (Edinburgh: T&T Clark, 1968), pp. 738–51.
27. For a helpful survey of the perils and promise of Trinitarian political theologies see Kathryn Tanner, 'Trinity', in *The Blackwell Companion to Political Theology*, ed. William T. Cavanaugh and Peter Scott (Malden: Blackwell, 2007), pp. 319–32.
28. David S. Cunningham, *These Three are One: The Practice of Trinitarian Theology* (Oxford: Blackwell, 1998), p. 243.
29. As of the time of writing, this report, entitled 'God the Trinity and the Unity of Humanity: Christian Monotheism and its Opposition to Violence', is available only in Italian. An introductory presentation, from which the quote was taken, is available online at: http://www.vatican.va/roman_curia/congregations/cfaith/cti_documents/rc_cti_20140117_monoteismo-cristiano_en.html (accessed 26 Feb. 2013).

5. Speaking of God

1. Augustine, *Sermons* 51-94, vol. III/3, trans. Edmund Hill, OP (New York: New City Press, 1991), p. 57 [Sermon 52.16].
2. Augustine, *On Christian Teaching*, trans. R.P.H. Green (New York: Oxford University Press, 1997), pp. 10–11.
3. Hans Urs von Balthasar, *Theo-Logic II: Truth of God*, trans. Adrian J. Walker (San Francisco: Ignatius Press, 2004), p. 280.
4. For a very helpful introduction to this distinction, upon which we have drawn in this section, see Robert Sokolowski, *The God of Faith and Reason: Foundations of Christian Theology* (Washington, DC: Catholic University of America Press, 1995), especially pp. 1–40.
5. Augustine, *Confessions*, trans. Henry Chadwick (New York: Oxford University Press, 1991), p. 69 [Book IV.xvi.29].
6. Augustine, *Confessions*, pp. 123–4 [Book VII.x.16].
7. This cosmology is helpfully narrated in Plato, 'Timaeus', in *Plato: Complete Works*, ed. John M. Cooper (Indianapolis: Hackett, 1997), pp. 1224–91. This work became something of a touchstone, was undoubtedly read by Augustine, and had a profound influence on the 'books of the Platonists' that emerged in late antiquity and throughout the Middle Ages.
8. Maximus the Confessor, *Selected Writings*, trans. George Charles Berthold (New York: Paulist, 1985), p. 65. During his exile, Maximus had his tongue cut so he could not speak and his right hand cut off so he could no longer write. He is given the name 'confessor' because he suffered for the faith yet was not directly martyred.
9. Thomas Aquinas, *Selected Philosophical Writings*, trans. Timothy McDermott (New York: Oxford University Press, 1993), pp. 214–30 [*Summa Theologiae* 1a.13].
10. Aquinas, *Selected Philosophical Writings*, p. 225 [*Summa Theologiae* 1a.13.5].
11. David Burrell, *Aquinas: God and Action* (Notre Dame: University of Notre Dame Press, 1979), p. 115.
12. Herbert McCabe, OP, *God Matters* (Springfield: Templegate Publishers, 1991), p. 177.
13. Aquinas, *Selected Philosophical Writings*, p. 216 [*Summa Theologiae* Ia.13.1, ad. 1, translation modified].
14. Jürgen Moltmann, *God in Creation: A New Theology of Creation and the Spirit of God*, trans. Margaret Kohl (Minneapolis: Fortress Press, 1993), p. xiii.

[15] Dietrich Bonhoeffer, *No Rusty Swords: Letters, Lectures and Notes from the Collected Works of Dietrich Bonhoeffer*, trans. Edwin H. Robertson and John Bowden (London: Fontana, 1965), p. 161.
[16] Stanley Hauerwas, *The Peaceable Kingdom: A Primer in Christian Ethics* (Notre Dame: University of Notre Dame Press, 1983), p. 59.
[17] Grace M. Jantzen, *Violence to Eternity* (London: Routledge, 2009), p. 7.
[18] Aquinas describes this with admirable clarity in Aquinas, *Selected Philosophical Writings*, pp. 251–62 [De potentia III.1-3].
[19] Rowan Williams, *On Christian Theology* (Oxford: Blackwell, 2000), p. 68.
[20] Williams, *On Christian Theology*, p. 78.

6. God, Faith and Knowledge

[1] J. Stevenson, ed. *A New Eusebius* (London: SPCK, 1963), pp. 298–99.
[2] This prayer is often called the Shema, the Hebrew word that translates as the imperative 'Hear'.
[3] See Chapter 7.
[4] This phrase is part of the parting address of John Robinson to the Pilgrims leaving on the Mayflower in 1620.
[5] See Roger E. van Harn, ed., *Exploring and Proclaiming the Apostles' Creed* (Grand Rapids: Eerdmans, 2004), p. x.
[6] For a very helpful way of telling this story see John D. Roth, *Stories: How Mennonites Came to Be* (Scottdale: Herald Press, 2006), pp. 65–85.
[7] See Brad S. Gregory, *The Unintended Reformation: How a Religious Revolution Secularized Society* (Cambridge: Harvard University Press, 2012).
[8] See Alan Kreider, *Worship and Evangelism in Pre-Christendom* (Cambridge: Grove Books, 1995), pp. 21–3. For a more extensive treatment see Alan Kreider, *Patient Ferment: The Growth of the Church in the Roman Empire* (Grand Rapids: Baker Academic, forthcoming in 2016), ch. 6.
[9] For the outstanding expression of the argument we are advancing here see Ellen T. Charry, *By the Renewing of Your Minds: The Pastoral Function of Christian Doctrine* (Oxford: Oxford University Press, 1997).
[10] See Brian Haymes, *The Concept of the Knowledge of God* (New York: St. Martins Press, 1988).
[11] As quoted in Walter Klassen, ed., *Anabaptism in Outline: Selected Primary Sources* (Scottdale: Herald Press, 1981), p. 87.

12. John H. Yoder, ed., *The Schleitheim Confession* (Scottdale: Herald Press, 1977).
13. Faith Bowers, *A Bold Experiment: The Story of Bloomsbury Chapel and Bloomsbury Central Baptist Church 1848–1999* (London: Bloomsbury Central Baptist Church, 1999), p. 93.

7. Experience of God

1. Frederick Buechner, *Beyond Worlds* (New York: Harper Collins, 2004), p. 131.
2. Karl Popper, *The Logic of Scientific Discovery* (London: Hutchinson, 1959), p. 280.
3. In book form see Martin Sixsmith, *Philomena* (London: Pan Books, 2010).
4. See Augustine, *Confessions*, trans. Henry Chadwick (New York: Oxford University Press, 1991), pp. 152–3.
5. The story is retold in Henry D. Rack, *Radical Enthusiast: John Wesley and the Rise of Methodism* (Philadelphia: Trinity Press International, 1989), p. 144.
6. Richard J. Foster, *Streams of Living Water: Celebrating the Great Traditions of Christian Faith* (San Francisco: Harper Collins, 1998), p. 63. This volume is a very valuable resource with many illustrations of the theme of this chapter.
7. The fullest treatment of Farmer's work is Christopher H. Partridge, *H.H. Farmer's Theological Interpretation of Religion: Towards a Personalist Theology of Religions* (Lampeter: Edwin Mellen Press, 1998).
8. See for example his poem, 'Stations on the Road to Freedom' in Dietrich Bonhoeffer, *Letters and Papers from Prison* (London: SCM, 1967), pp. 370–71.
9. Farmer's full discussion of these matters can be found in H.H. Farmer, *The World and God: A Study of Prayer, Providence and Miracle in Christian Experience* (London: Nisbet and Co., 1935), 13-31.
10. H.H. Farmer, *Towards Belief in God* (London: SCM Press, 1942), p. 40.
11. This has been a matter of some urgent discussion recently. For a survey of some of the issues involved see David Hilborn, Derek Tidball and Justin Thacker, eds, *The Atonement Debate: Papers from the London Symposium on the Theology of Atonement* (Grand Rapids: Zondervan, 2008).

[12] A very helpful discussion of these matters can be found in Douglas John Hall, *The Cross in our Context: Jesus and the Suffering World* (Minneapolis: Fortress Press, 2003).

[13] Here we are drawing heavily on John Townroe, 'Christian Spirituality and the Future of Man', in *Spirituality for Today: Papers from the 1967 Parish and People Conference*, ed. Eric James; London (SCM Press, 1968), pp. 41–55.

8. God and Evil

[1] For more on this see David Bentley Hart, *The Doors of the Sea: Where Was God in the Tsunami?* (Grand Rapids: Eerdmans, 2005), pp. 25–35.

[2] Augustine, *Confessions* (trans. Henry Chadwick; New York: Oxford University Press, 1991), pp. 124–5 [Book VII.xii].

[3] Augustine, *Confessions*, p. 15 [Book I.xiii.19].

[4] Augustine, *Confessions*, pp. 12–13 [Book I.x.16].

[5] Augustine, *Confessions*, p. 29 [Book II.iv.9].

[6] Augustine, *Confessions*, p. 33 [Book II.viii.16].

[7] This way of putting the matter can be seen in Rowan Williams, 'Insubstantial Evil', in *Augustine and His Critics*, ed. Robert Dodaro and George Lawless (London: Routledge, 2000), pp. 120–21.

[8] Augustine, *Confessions*, p. 112 [Book VII.i.2].

[9] Augustine, *Confessions*, pp. 119–21 [Book VII.vii.11-viii.12].

[10] Augustine, *Confessions*, pp. 115–16 [Book VII.v.7].

[11] For a helpful account of the significant differences and shifts see Kenneth Surin, *Theology and the Problem of Evil* (Oxford: Blackwell, 1986), especially pp. 1–37.

[12] See Immanuel Kant, 'Religion Within the Bounds of Mere Reason', in *Religion and Rational Theology*, ed. Allen W. Wood and George di Giovanni (Cambridge: Cambridge University Press, 1996), pp. 69–97.

[13] Hannah Arendt, '"What Remains? The Language Remains": A Conversation with Günter Gaus', in *Hannah Arendt: Essays in Understanding, 1930–1954*, ed. Jerome Kohn (New York: Harcourt, Brace & Co., 1994), p. 14. Perhaps not incidentally, Arendt's doctoral work investigated the concept of love in Augustine so she was familiar with the Christian tradition of thinking about evil.

[14] Jürgen Moltmann, *The Experiment Hope*. trans. M. Douglas Meeks (London: SCM, 1975), p. 73. Christian theologians would be well

advised to tread carefully here because it is a very short step to appropriate for uniquely Christian purposes what was primarily, though not exclusively, an event of Jewish suffering.

15. Dorothee Sölle, *Christ the Representative: An Essay in Theology after the 'Death of God'*, trans. David Lewis (London: SCM, 1967), p. 121.
16. Jürgen Moltmann, *The Crucified God*, trans. R. Wilson and J. Bowden (London: SCM Press, 2001), pp. 145–53.
17. Moltmann, *Crucified God*, p. 274.
18. Dietrich Bonhoeffer, *Letters and Papers from Prison* (London: SCM, 1967), p. 197.
19. Gustavo Gutiérrez, *Essential Writings*, ed. James B. Nickoloff (London: SCM Press, 1996), p. 318.
20. Paul S. Fiddes, *The Creative Suffering of God* (Oxford: Clarendon Press, 1988), p. 20.
21. Fiddes, *Creative Suffering of God*, p. 17.
22. Moltmann, *Crucified God*, p. 202.
23. Moltmann, *Crucified God*, p. 192.
24. Moltmann, *Crucified God*, p. 230.
25. For a brief yet helpful account of this shift see Ronald Goetz, 'The Suffering God: The Rise of a New Orthodoxy,' *Christian Century* 103 (1986): pp. 385–9.
26. Cyril of Alexandria, *Cyril of Alexandria: Select Letters*, trans. Lionel R. Wickham (Oxford: Clarendon Press, 1983), p. 123.
27. See Thomas G. Weinandy, *Does God Suffer?* (Notre Dame: University of Notre Dame Press, 2000), especially pp. 172–213.
28. Indeed, in the writing of this book the passibility/impassibility debate is the point at which we have found ourselves wrestling with each other most. For an extremely helpful collection of essays that engages this debate see James F. Keating and Thomas Joseph White, eds, *Divine Impassibility and the Mystery of Human Suffering* (Grand Rapids: Eerdmans, 2009).
29. Alfred North Whitehead, *Process and Reality*, ed. David Ray Griffin and Donald W. Sherburne (New York: Free Press, 1978), p. 351.
30. Paul Imhof and Hubert Biallowons, eds, *Karl Rahner in Dialogue: Conversations and Interviews* (New York: Crossroad,1986), pp. 126–7.
31. For one clear example of this see Jürgen Moltmann, *The Future of Creation*, trans. Margaret Kohl (London: SCM Press, 1979), pp. 59–79.
32. Anselm, *The Major Works*, ed. Brian Davies and G. R. Evans (New York: Oxford University Press, 1998), 91 [*Proslogion* 8].

[33] Augustine, *Concerning the City of God against the Pagans*, trans. Henry Bettenson (London: Penguin Books, 2003), pp. 564–5 [Book XIV.9].
[34] David Bentley Hart, 'No Shadow of Turning: On Divine Impassibility,' *Pro Ecclesia* 11/ 2 (2002): p. 200.
[35] Hart, 'No Shadow of Turning', p. 191.
[36] For a lucid account of Julian's thought in this respect see Grace M. Jantzen, *Julian of Norwich* (London: SPCK, 2000), especially pp. 167–202.
[37] As cited in Jantzen, *Julian of Norwich*, p. 183.
[38] Julian of Norwich, *Revelations of Divine Love*, trans. Elizabeth Spearing (London: Penguin, 1998), p. 22.

9. God in History

[1] Charles Péguy, *The Portal of the Mystery of Hope*, trans. David Louis Schindler, Jr. (Grand Rapids: Eerdmans, 1996), pp. 7–11.
[2] Terry Eagleton, *The Illusions of Postmodernism* (Oxford: Blackwell, 1996), p. vii.
[3] Oliver O'Donovan, *The Desire of the Nations: Rediscovering the Roots of Political Theology* (New York: Cambridge University Press, 1999), p. 21.
[4] Walter Brueggemann, 'Always in the Shadow of the Empire,' in *The Church as Counterculture*, ed. Michael L. Budde and Robert W. Brimlow (Albany: SUNY, 2000), p. 48.
[5] For an extrapolation of this see Hendrik Berkhof, *Christ and the Powers*, trans. John Howard Yoder (Scottdale: Herald Press, 1977).
[6] John Howard Yoder, *The Politics of Jesus: Vicit Agnus Noster* (Grand Rapids: Eerdmans, 2nd edn, 1998), pp. 232–3.
[7] John Howard Yoder, *The War of the Lamb: The Ethics of Nonviolence and Peacemaking*, ed. Glen Stassen, Mark Thiessen Nation, and Matt Hamsher (Grand Rapids: Brazos Press, 2009), p. 41.
[8] Hans Urs von Balthasar, *A Theology of History* (San Francisco: Ignatius Press, 1994), p. 37.
[9] John Howard Yoder, *He Came Preaching Peace* (Scottdale: Herald Press, 2004), p. 29.
[10] Yoder, *War of the Lamb*, p. 85.
[11] John Howard Yoder, *Nevertheless: The Varieties and Shortcomings of Religious Pacifism* (Scottdale: Herald Press, rev. edn, 1992), p. 137.
[12] John H. Yoder, ed., 'Armaments and Eschatology', *Studies in Christian Ethics* 1/1 (1988): p. 56.

[13] John Howard Yoder, *Nonviolence – A Brief History: The Warsaw Lectures*, ed. Paul Martens, Matthew Porter and Myles Werntz (Waco: Baylor University Press, 2010), p. 43.

[14] John Howard Yoder, *The Royal Priesthood: Essays Ecclesiological and Ecumenical*, ed. Michael Cartwright (Grand Rapids: Eerdmans, 1994), p. 129.

[15] Yoder, *Royal Priesthood*, pp. 137–8.

[16] Elie Wiesel, 'Art and Culture After the Holocaust', in *Auschwitz: Beginning of a New Era?*, ed. Eva Fleischner (New York: KTAV, 1977), p. 403.

[17] Dorothy Day, *The Long Loneliness* (New York: Harper Collins, 1997), p. 43.

[18] Day, *Long Loneliness*, p. 107.

[19] Day, *Long Loneliness*, p. 150.

[20] Dorothy Day, *Loaves and Fishes* (New York: Harper and Row, 1963), 204.

[21] Patrick G. Coy, 'Beyond the Ballot Box: The Catholic Worker Movement and Nonviolent Direct Action', in *Dorothy Day and the Catholic Worker Movement*, ed. William Thorn, Philip Runkel and Susan Mountin (Milwaukee: Marquette University Press, 2001), p. 183.

[22] Yoder, *Nonviolence*, p. 113.

[23] Dorothy Day, 'Aims and Purposes', *The Catholic Worker* (February 1940), p. 7. Accessed from the Dorothy Day Library online at http://dorothyday.catholicworker.org/articles/182.html (accessed 25 Apr. 2014).

[24] John Howard Yoder, *Body Politics: Five Practices for the Christian Church Before the Watching World* (Scottdale: Herald Press, 2001), p. ix.

[25] Yoder, *Body Politics*, pp. 20–21.

[26] William T. Cavanaugh, *Torture and Eucharist: Theology, Politics, and the Body of Christ* (Malden: Blackwell, 1998), p. 269.

[27] William T. Cavanaugh, *Being Consumed: Economics and Christian Desire* (Grand Rapids: Eerdmans, 2008), pp. 53–8.

Conclusion

[1] As quoted in Eberhard Bethge, *Dietrich Bonhoeffer: A Biography* (Minneapolis: Fortress Press, 2000), p. 236.

Bibliography

Addley, Esther. 'Atheist SundayAssembly branches out in first wave of expansion.' The Guardian (2013), http://www.theguardian.com/world/2013/sep/14/atheist-sunday-assembly-branches-out.

Anselm. *The Major Works*. Edited by Brian Davies and G. R. Evans. New York: Oxford University Press, 1998.

Aquinas, Thomas. *Selected Philosophical Writings*. Translated by Timothy McDermott. New York: Oxford University Press, 1993.

Arendt, Hannah. '"What Remains? The Language Remains": A Conversation with Günter Gaus.' In *Hannah Arendt: Essays in Understanding*, 1930–1954, edited by Jerome Kohn, 1–23. New York: Harcourt, Brace & Co., 1994.

Aristotle. 'Physics.' In *The Complete Works of Aristotle*, edited by Jonathan Barnes, 315-446. Princeton: Princeton University Press, 1984.

Augustine. *Confessions*. Translated by Henry Chadwick. New York: Oxford University Press, 1991.

———. *Sermons 51–94*. Translated by Edmund Hill, O.P. Vol. III/3. New York: New City Press, 1991.

———. *On Christian Teaching*. Translated by R. P. H. Green. New York: Oxford University Press, 1997.

———. *Concerning the City of God against the Pagans*. Translated by Henry Bettenson. London: Penguin Books, 2003.

———. *The Trinity*. Translated by Edmund Hill, O.P. Second ed. New York: New City Press, 2012.

Ayres, Lewis. *Nicaea and its Legacy: An Approach to Fourth-Century Trinitarian Theology*. New York: Oxford University Press, 2004.

Balthasar, Hans Urs von. *Truth is Symphonic: Aspects of Christian Pluralism*. Translated by Graham Harrison. San Francisco: Ignatius Press, 1987.

———. *A Theology of History*. San Francisco: Ignatius Press, 1994.

———. *Theo-Logic II: Truth of God*. Translated by Adrian J. Walker. San Francisco: Ignatius Press, 2004.

Basil of Caesarea. 'Letter CLIX.' In *Nicene and Post-Nicene Fathers*, edited by Philip Schaff and Henry Wace, 613–14. Edinburgh: T&T Clark, 1994.

———. "Letter XXXVIII." In *Nicene and Post-Nicene Fathers*, edited by Philip Schaff and Henry Wace, 426–33. Edinburgh: T&T Clark, 1994.

Berkhof, Hendrik. *Christ and the Powers*. Translated by John Howard Yoder. Scottdale: Herald Press, 1977.

Bethge, Eberhard. *Dietrich Bonhoeffer: A Biography*. Revised ed. Minneapolis: Fortress Press, 2000.

Bonhoeffer, Dietrich. *No Rusty Swords: Letters, Lectures and Notes from the Collected Works of Dietrich Bonhoeffer*. Translated by Edwin H. Robertson and John Bowden. London: Fontana, 1965.

———. *Letters and Papers From Prison*. London: SCM, 1967.

Bowers, Faith. *A Bold Experiment: The Story of Bloomsbury Chapel and Bloomsbury Central Baptist Church 1848–1999*. London: Bloomsbury Central Baptist Church, 1999.

Brueggemann, Walter. "The Prophet as Destabilizing Presence." In *The Pastor as Prophet*, edited by Earl E. Shelp and Ronald H. Sunderland. New York: The Pilgrim Press, 1985.

———. 'Always in the Shadow of the Empire.' In *The Church as Counterculture*, edited by Michael L. Budde and Robert W. Brimlow, 39–58. Albany: SUNY, 2000.

Buechner, Frederick. *Beyond Words*. New York: Harper Collins, 2004.

Burgess, Walter H. *The Pastor of the Pilgrims: A Biography of John Robinson*. New York: Harcourt, Brace & Howe, 1920.

Burrell, David. *Aquinas: God and Action*. Notre Dame: University of Notre Dame Press, 1979.

Cavanaugh, William T. *Torture and Eucharist: Theology, Politics, and the Body of Christ*. Malden: Blackwell, 1998.

———. *Being Consumed: Economics and Christian Desire*. Grand Rapids: Eerdmans, 2008.

Charry, Ellen T. *By the Renewing of Your Minds: The Pastoral Function of Christian Doctrine*. Oxford: Oxford University Press, 1997.
Chesterton, G. K. *St. Thomas Aquinas*. San Rafael: Angelico Press, 2011.
Cochrane, Arthur C., ed. *Reformed Confessions of the 16th Century*. Philadelphia: Westminster, 1966.
Coy, Patrick G. 'Beyond the Ballot Box: The Catholic Worker Movement and Nonviolent Direct Action.' In *Dorothy Day and the Catholic Worker Movement*, edited by William Thorn, Philip Runkel and Susan Mountin, 169–83. Milwaukee: Marquette University Press, 2001.
Cunningham, David S. *These Three are One: The Practice of Trinitarian Theology*. Oxford: Blackwell, 1998.
Cyril of Alexandria. *Cyril of Alexandria: Select Letters*. Translated by Lionel R. Wickham. Oxford: Clarendon Press, 1983.
Davy, Charles. 'The Earthquake at Lisbon, 1755.' *Modern History Sourcebook*, http://www.fordham.edu/halsall/mod/1755lisbonquake.asp.
Day, Dorothy. *Loaves and Fishes*. New York: Harper and Row, 1963.
———. *The Long Loneliness*. New York: Harper Collins, 1997.
de Botton, Alain. *Religion for Atheists: A Non-Believer's Guide to the Uses of Religion*. London: Penguin, 2013.
Driver, John. *Radical Faith: An Alternative History of the Christian Church*. Kitchener: Pandora Press, 1999.
Eagleton, Terry. *The Illusions of Postmodernism*. Oxford: Blackwell, 1996.
Eliot, T.S. *Murder in the Cathedral*. London: Faber and Faber, 1965.
Farmer, H.H. *The World and God: A Study of Prayer, Providence and Miracle in Christian Experience*. London: Nisbet and Co., 1935.
———. *Towards Belief in God*. London: SCM Press, 1942.
Fiddes, Paul S. *The Creative Suffering of God*. Oxford: Clarendon Press, 1988.
Foster, Richard J. *Streams of Living Water: Celebrating the Great Traditions of Christian Faith*. San Francisco: Harper Collins, 1998.
Goetz, Ronald. 'The Suffering God: The Rise of a New Orthodoxy.' *Christian Century* 103, (1986): 385-89.
Gregory, Brad S. *The Unintended Reformation: How a Religious Revolution Secularized Society*. Cambridge: Harvard University Press, 2012.

Gregory of Nyssa. 'Homilies on Ecclesiastes.' In *Gregory of Nyssa: Homilies on Ecclesiastes*, edited by Stuart George Hall, 31–144. Berlin: W. de Gruyter, 1993.

———. 'On the Holy Spirit.' In *Nicene and Post-Nicene Fathers*, edited by Philip Schaff and Henry Wace, 588–607. Edinburgh: T&T Clark, 1994.

Gutiérrez, Gustavo. *Essential Writings*. Edited by James B. Nickoloff. London: SCM Press, 1996.

Hall, Douglas John. *The Cross in our Context: Jesus and the Suffering World*. Minneapolis: Fortress Press, 2003.

Hart, David Bentley. 'No Shadow of Turning: On Divine Impassibility.' *Pro Ecclesia* 11, no. 2 (2002): 184-206.

———. *The Doors of the Sea: Where Was God in the Tsunami?* Grand Rapids: Eerdmans, 2005.

Hauerwas, Stanley. *The Peaceable Kingdom: A Primer in Christian Ethics*. Notre Dame: University of Notre Dame Press, 1983.

Haymes, Brian. *The Concept of the Knowledge of God*. New York: St. Martins Press, 1988.

———. 'Thomas Helwys' The Mystery of Iniquity: Is it Still Relevant in the Twenty-First Century?' In *Exploring Baptist Origins*, edited by Anthony R. Cross and Nicholas J. Wood, 61–77. Oxford: Regent's Park College, 2010.

Helwys, Thomas. *A Short Declaration of the Mystery of Iniquity*. London: The Baptist Historical Society, 1935.

Hilborn, David, Derek Tidball, and Justin Thacker, eds. *The Atonement Debate: Papers from the London Symposium on the Theology of Atonement*. Grand Rapids: Zondervan, 2008.

Imhof, Paul, and Hubert Biallowons, eds. *Karl Rahner in Dialogue: Conversations and Interviews*. New York: Crossroad, 1986.

Jantzen, Grace M. *Julian of Norwich*. London: SPCK, 2000.

———. *Violence to Eternity*. London: Routledge, 2009.

Julian of Norwich. *Revelations of Divine Love*. Translated by Elizabeth Spearing. London: Penguin, 1998.

Kant, Immanuel. 'Religion Within the Bounds of Mere Reason.' In *Religion and Rational Theology*, edited by Allen W. Wood and George di Giovanni, 57–213. Cambridge: Cambridge University Press, 1996.

———. 'The Conflict of the Faculties.' In *Religion and Rational Theology*, edited by Allen W. Wood and George di Giovanni, 233–328. Cambridge: Cambridge University Press, 2001.

Keating, James F., and Thomas Joseph White, eds. *Divine Impassibility and the Mystery of Human Suffering*. Grand Rapids: Eerdmans, 2009.

Klassen, Walter, ed. *Anabaptism in Outline: Selected Primary Sources*. Scottdale: Herald Press, 1981.

Kreider, Alan. *Worship and Evangelism in Pre-Christendom*. Cambridge: Grove Books, 1995.

———. *Patient Ferment: The Growth of the Church in the Roman Empire*. Grand Rapids: Baker Academic, forthcoming in 2016.

Leithart, Peter J. *Defending Constantine: The Twilight of an Empire and the Dawn of Christendom*. Downers Grove: InterVarsity Press, 2010.

Maximus the Confessor. *Selected Writings*. Translated by George Charles Berthold. New York: Paulist, 1985.

McCabe, Herbert, OP. *God Matters*. Springfield: Templegate Publishers, 1991.

———. *God Still Matters*. London: Continuum, 2002.

Moltmann, Jürgen. *The Experiment Hope*. Translated by M. Douglas Meeks. London: SCM, 1975.

———. *The Future of Creation*. Translated by Margaret Kohl. London: SCM Press, 1979.

———. *God in Creation: A New Theology of Creation and the Spirit of God*. Translated by Margaret Kohl. Minneapolis: Fortress Press, 1993.

———. *The Crucified God*. Translated by R. Wilson and J. Bowden. London: SCM Press, 2001.

Newell, Tim. *Forgiving Justice: A Quaker Vision for Criminal Justice*. London: Quaker Home Service, 2000.

Newman, John Henry Cardinal. *An Essay on the Development of Christian Doctrine*. Sixth ed. Notre Dame: University of Notre Dame Press, 1989.

O'Donovan, Oliver. *The Desire of the Nations: Rediscovering the Roots of Political Theology*. New York: Cambridge University Press, 1999.

Partridge, Christopher H. *H.H. Farmer's Theological Interpretation of Religion: Towards a Personalist Theology of Religions*. Lampeter: Edwin Mellen Press, 1998.

Péguy, Charles. *The Portal of the Mystery of Hope*. Translated by David Louis Schindler, Jr. Grand Rapids: Eerdmans, 1996.

Plato. 'Timaeus.' In *Plato: Complete Works*, edited by John M. Cooper, 1224–91. Indianapolis: Hackett, 1997.

Popper, Karl. *The Logic of Scientific Discovery*. London: Hutchinson, 1959.

Rack, Henry D. *Radical Enthusiast: John Wesley and the Rise of Methodism*. Philadelphia: Trinity Press International, 1989.

Reimer, A. James. 'Mennonites, Christ, and Culture: The Yoder Legacy.' In *Mennonites and Classical Theology: Dogmatic Foundations for Christian Ethics*, 288–99. Kitchener: Pandora Press, 2001.

Robinson, Marilynne. *When I was a Child I Read Books*. New York: Picador, 2012.

Roth, John D. *Stories: How Mennonites Came to Be*. Scottdale: Herald Press, 2006.

Schleiermacher, Friedrich. *The Christian Faith*. Translated by H. R. Mackintosh and J. S. Stewart. Edinburgh: T & T Clark, 1968.

Sixsmith, Martin. *Philomena*. London: Pan Books, 2010.

Sokolowski, Robert. *The God of Faith and Reason: Foundations of Christian Theology*. Washington, D.C.: The Catholic University of America Press, 1995.

Sölle, Dorothee. *Christ the Representative: An Essay in Theology after the 'Death of God'*. Translated by David Lewis. London: SCM, 1967.

Stevenson, J., ed. *A New Eusebius*. London: SPCK, 1963.

Surin, Kenneth. *Theology and the Problem of Evil*. Oxford: Blackwell, 1986.

Tanner, Kathryn. 'Trinity.' In T*he Blackwell Companion to Political Theology*, edited by William T. Cavanaugh and Peter Scott, 319-32. Malden: Blackwell, 2007.

Townroe, John. 'Christian Spirituality and the Future of Man.' In *Spirituality for Today: Papers from the 1967 Parish and People Conference*, edited by Eric James, 41-55. London: SCM Press, 1968.

van Harn, Roger E., ed. *Exploring and Proclaiming the Apostles' Creed*. Grand Rapids: Eerdmans, 2004.

Voltaire. *The Works of Voltaire: The Lisbon Earthquake and Other Poems*, ed. by Tobias George Smollett, et. al. Vol. XXVI (Akron: The Werner Company), 1901.

Weinandy, Thomas G. *Does God Suffer?* Notre Dame: University of Notre Dame Press, 2000.

Wells, Samuel. *Improvisation: The Drama of Christian Ethics*. Grand Rapids: Brazos Press, 2004.

Whitehead, Alfred North. *Process and Reality*. Edited by David Ray Griffin and Donald W. Sherburne. New York: The Free Press, 1978.
Wiesel, Elie. 'Art and Culture After the Holocaust.' In *Auschwitz: Beginning of a New Era?*, edited by Eva Fleischner, 403–16. New York: KTAV, 1977.
Williams, Daniel H. 'Constantine and the "Fall" of the Church.' In *Christian Origins: Theology, Rhetoric and Community*, edited by Lewis Ayres and Gareth Jones, 117–36. New York: Routledge, 1998.
Williams, Rowan. 'Insubstantial Evil.' In *Augustine and His Critics*, edited by Robert Dodaro and George Lawless, 105–23. London: Routledge, 2000.
———. *On Christian Theology*. Oxford: Blackwell, 2000.
———. *Arius: Heresy and Tradition*. 2nd ed. London: SCM, 2001.
Wittgenstein, Ludwig. *Culture and Value*. Translated by Peter Winch. Revised ed. Oxford: Blackwell, 1998.
Yoder, John H., ed. *The Schleitheim Confession*. Scottdale: Herald Press, 1977.
———. 'Armaments and Eschatology.' *Studies in Christian Ethics* 1, no. 1 (1988): 43-61.
Yoder, John Howard. 'The Constantinian Sources of Western Social Ethics.' In *The Priestly Kingdom: Social Ethics as Gospel*, 135–47. Notre Dame: University of Notre Dame Press, 1984.
———. *Nevertheless: The Varieties and Shortcomings of Religious Pacifism*. Revised ed. Scottdale: Herald Press, 1992.
———. *The Royal Priesthood: Essays Ecclesiological and Ecumenical*. Edited by Michael Cartwright. Grand Rapids: Eerdmans, 1994.
———. *The Politics of Jesus: Vicit Agnus Noster*. Second ed. Grand Rapids: Eerdmans, 1998.
———. *Body Politics: Five Practices for the Christian Church Before the Watching World*. Scottdale: Herald Press, 2001.
———. *Preface to Theology: Christology and Theological Method*. Grand Rapids: Brazos, 2002.
———. *The Original Revolution: Essays on Christian Pacifism*. Scottdale: Herald Press, 2003.
———. *He Came Preaching Peace*. Scottdale: Herald Press, 2004.
———. *The War of the Lamb: The Ethics of Nonviolence and Peacemaking*. Edited by Glen Stassen, Mark Thiessen Nation and Matt Hamsher. Grand Rapids: Brazos Press, 2009.

———. *Nonviolence–A Brief History: The Warsaw Lectures*. Edited by Paul Martens, Matthew Porter and Myles Werntz. Waco: Baylor University Press, 2010.

———. *Revolutionary Christianity: The 1966 South American Lectures*. Edited by Paul Martens, Mark Thiessen Nation, Matthew Porter and Myles Werntz. Eugene: Cascade, 2011.

Zehr, Howard. *The Little Book of Restorative Justice*. Intercourse: Good Books, 2002.

Index

Anabaptist(s) 56, 94, 98–9
analogy 65, 70–1, 83–4
Anselm of Canterbury 127
Alexander 66
apocalyptic 134–7
Aquinas, Thomas 6, 65, 81–4
Arendt, Hannah 121
Arius 66
Aristotle 61
atheism (atheist) 4, 82, 118
Augustine, Saint 63, 65, 66, 72, 75, 77–80, 110, 119–20, 127
Auschwitz 121–3

Balthasar, Hans Urs von 77, 135–6
baptism 3, 29–30, 51, 69, 94–5, 140
Barth, Karl 43, 61
Basil of Caesarea 69–70
Bible (biblical) 5–6, 11–7, 19, 21, 26, 28, 36, 41, 44–5, 49, 55–7, 76, 89, 91–2, 94–7, 99, 106, 108–10, 123, 127–8, 132–5, 143–5
and the Trinity 61–2, 64–6, 68–9
Blaurock, George 94
Bloomsbury Central Baptist Church 100

Bonhoeffer, Dietrich 43, 86, 112, 123, 145
Botton, Alain de 4
Brueggemann, Walter 133
Buechner, Frederick 105

Calvin, John 93
Cappadocian Fathers 39, 69–70
Chesterton, G.K. 6, 7
christendom 2–5, 12–15, 28, 41, 62, 87
church 3–6, 13–14, 31, 40–3, 47, 49–55, 57, 61–2, 65, 67–8, 77, 90, 92–101, 107, 110, 114–7, 132, 138, 140–1, 142–4
Communion (see also Eucharist) 68, 93, 138, 146
constantinianism (Constantine) 2–3, 5, 39–40, 62, 67, 90, 149n.5
Council of Nicaea 66–70
creation 2, 7, 13–16, 26, 32, 34–5, 56–7, 63, 81–8, 116, 125–8, 132–3, 135–6, 139
creatures (creaturely) 76, 80–8, 98, 119–123, 143
creeds 62, 68, 93, 99
Cyril of Alexandria 126

Davy, Charles 1
Day, Dorothy 138–140
Denck, Hans 98
Didsbury Baptist Church 100
discipleship 2, 7, 47, 55, 62–4, 66, 69, 72, 84, 92, 94, 101, 116, 135, 142
doctrine(s) (*see also* Trinity) 36–7, 42, 48, 61–6, 68–73, 85–6, 98–9, 114–5, 140
   development of 6, 13, 63–6, 69–70
   of God 5–6, 13, 48, 115, 119, 129

economics 6, 21, 24, 53, 72–73, 86, 96, 133, 141
eschatology 52, 73, 131–134
Eucharist (*see also* Communion) 93, 141
evil 3, 6, 19, 22, 53, 78, 118–23, 127–130, 135, 138–9
experience of God 5–6, 11, 97, 105–17

Farmer, Herbert Henry 111–3
Fiddes, Paul 125
Fox, George 56
Francis of Assisi, Saint 6–7, 56, 65

German Christians (*Deutsche Christien*) 42, 85
Gomez, Maria Christina 100
Grebel, Conrad 94
Gregory of Nyssa 39, 69–71, 149n.5
Gutiérrez, Gustavo 123

Hart, David Bentley 128
Hauerwas, Stanley 86
Helwys, Thomas 41–2

Hitler, Adolf 42, 85, 122
hope 6, 23, 34, 57, 64, 95, 114, 122–3, 128, 130, 131–133, 136–146

incarnation, doctrine of 34–7, 77, 96, 100, 123, 125–6
injustice (*see also* justice) 24, 26, 109, 123
improvisation (*see also* Wells, Samuel) 55, 65–6, 68–9, 77

Jantzen, Grace M. 87
Jesus Christ 6, 14, 16, 27–31, 33–43, 46–53, 62, 69, 74, 76–8, 90, 93–101, 110, 112, 116, 123, 125–7, 134–7, 139–41, 144
   as disturbing figure 31–3, 48
Julian of Norwich 129–30, 132, 157n.36
justice (*see also* injustice) 2, 4–5, 11, 21, 26, 37, 132, 138

Kant, Immanuel 72, 121
knowledge of God 89, 92, 97, 100, 102

Laplace, Pierre–Simon 142
Leibniz, Gottfried 121
love 12–13, 15, 18, 21, 25, 32, 34, 35, 38, 46, 53, 55, 57, 71–3, 79, 82, 88, 89, 91, 95–6, 98, 101–2, 111, 114–6, 119, 124–5, 128–9, 131, 135–6, 139–40, 142, 146

Machiavelli, Niccolò 4
Mantz, Felix 94
martyrdom (martyr, martyred) 28, 48–9, 94, 101, 112, 122, 152n.8
Maximus the Confessor 80, 152n.8

McCabe, Herbert 26, 84
monarchy 22–3, 26, 87, 133
Moltmann, Jürgen 122–3, 125, 129

Newman, John Henry 64–5
Niemöler, Martin 43
Nietzsche, Friedrich 4
non–violence (*see also* peace, violence) 74, 134, 136–9

O'Donovan, Oliver 5, 133

Palmer, Phoebe 110–1
peace (peacemaking, *see also* violence, non–violence) 7, 26, 32–3, 52, 72–4, 87, 102, 112, 132–4, 144
and the Trinity 72–4
Péguy, Charles 131
Plato (Platonists) 1, 79, 152n.7
politics 4, 13, 17–8, 23, 28, 62, 133–7, 144
Popper, Karl 105

Rahner, Karl 127
Reimer, A. James 5
Richard of Chichester 89
Robinson, John 56, 153n.4
Romero, Oscar 101

Sabellius 71
Schleiermacher, Friedrich 72
slavery (slaves, enslave) 11, 19–21, 39–40, 52–3, 100, 109, 124, 134, 145, 148n.4
sola scriptura 64, 92, 94
Sölle, Dorothee 122
sovereignty of God 3, 5, 11, 14, 16–7, 21, 23, 25, 33, 132, 134

Spirit (spirituality) 29, 36, 48–52, 61–3, 67–9, 71–2, 77, 88, 92–5, 98, 101–2, 111, 114, 137–8, 145–6
and Jesus 46–7
discernment of 54–6, 57
metaphors of 44–5
Stumpf, Simon 94
suffering (*see also* evil) 16, 25, 30, 34, 38, 116, 118, 121–30, 132, 134–6, 139, 155n.14

theodicy (*see also* evil, suffering) 121
Trinity, doctrine of 6, 13, 61–74, 115, 144–5
analogies of 70–2
and doctrine 63–6
and peacemaking 72–4, 151n.29

violence (*see also* non–violence, peace) 2, 17, 25, 73–4, 85–7, 90, 96, 121, 124, 129, 132, 134, 136–9, 145
Voltaire 1, 2, 4, 121

Wainwright, Geoffrey 93
Wells, Samuel 55, 65
Wesley, John 93, 110
Wiesel, Elie 137
Williams, Rowan 87
Wittgenstein, Ludwig 61–2
worship 7, 25–6, 41, 47, 57, 68–9, 72, 75, 93, 97, 101–2, 109, 113, 115, 142, 145

Yoder, John Howard 3, 5, 57, 62, 63, 134–7, 139–41, 149n.5

Zwingli, Ulrich 93–4

www.ingramcontent.com/pod-product-compliance
Lightning Source LLC
Chambersburg PA
CBHW030112170426
43198CB00009B/595